CURTAIN RECIPES

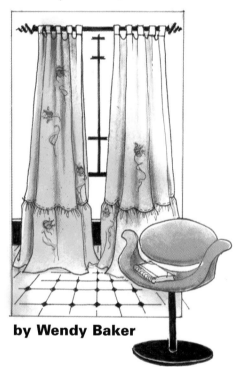

by Wendy Baker

First published in the United Kingdom in 2004

Shoestring Book Company
P.O.BOX 9044
Gloucester GL19 4ZR
United Kingdom

British Library Cataloguing-in-Publication Data. A record of this book is available from the British Library.

ISBN 0-9532939-5-5 (Book)
ISBN 0-9532939-6-3 (Cards)

Printed in the United Kingdom

Acknowledgments:
Wendy Baker would like to thank Chrissie Carriere for her lovely illustrations as usual, as well as her input and enthusiasm in all our projects over the years. And a special thank you to Wendy Cushing and Marian Cochrane for their help and encouragement. To Cath Kidston for the marvellous fabric on the cover.

Other books by Wendy Baker:
The Curtain Sketchbook   ISBN 0-9532939-2-0
Window and Bed Sketchbook   ISBN 0-953-293-947
Curtain and Fabric Selector   ISBN 1-85585-804-5

Don't get me wrong! I'm not against traditional curtains but having them for the sake of having them seems a bit of a futile exercise as well as an expensive one. Some windows are beautiful in their own right and it seems sad to cover them up, unless, of course, you have a view of the gasworks just outside, in which case cover up, but try to keep your window coverings simple. Simple is generally less expensive too, which is something we all need these days. Choose your fabrics carefully as a wrong decision can be costly, there's a fine line between the right look and the wrong look. When in doubt go for natural plain fabrics. You can always jazz them up with ribbons and various trimmings at the end.

I've tried to keep the designs uncomplicated and the same with the instructions – you don't need to have a degree in sewing to use these recipes but a bit of common sense always helps!

Making a Start

DON'T PANIC!

IT'S EASY WHEN YOU KNOW HOW. HAVE FUN MAKING YOUR
CURTAINS. CHOOSE A DESIGN FROM THE BOOK OR CARDS
AND FOLLOW THE ILLUSTRATED INSTRUCTIONS..

WHAT COULD BE EASIER?

Select the Right Design

CHECK IT OUT:

If you ARE LUCKy ENOUGH TO HAVE A LOVELY PERIOD WINDOW OR A WONDERFUL VIEW BE CAREFUL NOT TO BLOCK IT WITH CURTAINS, MAKE SURE THAT THEY STACK WELL BACK AT EACH SIDE AND DON'T COVER THE WINDOW.

1. BASIC WINDOWS – CHOOSE A BLIND OR EVEN SHORT CURTAINS SO AS NOT TO OVER POWER THE WINDOW.

2. RECESSED WINDOW – PERFECT FOR A TRANSLUCENT BLIND OR VOILE CAFÉ CURTAIN THEN YOU DON'T LOSE ANY LIGHT.

3. A ROUND WINDOW ALWAYS CAUSES PROBLEMS – DON'T CLUTTER IT – LEAVE IT PLAIN, YOU CAN ALWAYS "DRESS" THE WINDOW TO SUIT THE ROOM. (SEE PAGE 92)

4. YOU OFTEN FIND THIS SHAPE IN COTTAGES – SHORT CURTAINS WILL WORK BUT I PREFER LONG ONE'S. DON'T HAVE A VALANCE IT WILL LOOK TOO HEAVY.

5. 1930's METAL FRAME – GREAT SHAPE FOR CONTEMPORARY CURTAINS & PANELS. WORKS WELL WITH BLINDS TOO.

6. GEORGIAN WINDOWS – HAS TO BE MY FAVOURITE – LONG ELEGANT CURTAINS, A VALANCE, EVERYTHING LOOKS GOOD.

7. GEORGIAN ARCHED WINDOWS – MAKE SURE YOUR CURTAIN POLE IS IN THE RIGHT POSITION TO ALLOW CURTAINS TO STACK RIGHT BACK OR YOU WILL LOSE THE BEAUTY OF THIS WONDERFUL WINDOW.

8. DORMER WINDOWS – BEST TO HAVE PORTIÉRE PANELS. (SEE PAGE 114) OR BLINDS IF YOU CAN CLEAR THE WINDOW BY FIXING THEM AS HIGH AS POSSIBLE.

IMPORTANT TIPS:
1. DRAW YOUR WINDOW SHAPE ON GRAPH PAPER — WORK ON A SET SCALE, SAY 1 SQUARE = 10CM (4"). THIS WILL HELP YOU WORK OUT THE PROPORTIONS OF THE CURTAIN OR BLIND.

2. USE A RETRACTABLE METAL TAPE MEASURE.

1. MEASURING CURTAIN LENGTH

(A) SHORT CURTAINS, MEASURE FROM POLE OR TRACKING TO 15CM (6") BELOW SILL

(B) FOR LONG CURTAINS, MEASURE FROM POLE OR TRACKING TO FLOOR — ADD EXTRA IF CURTAINS BREAK ON THE FLOOR.

(C) PELMETS OR VALANCES (THE BOARD AND TRACKING IS FIXED IN THE SAME POSITION AS A POLE) SHOULD BE 1/6TH OF THE TOTAL LENGTH OF THE CURTAINS. DIVIDE THE TOTAL LENGTH OF THE CURTAINS BY 6 TO FIND LENGTH OF A STRAIGHT PELMET. ADD 15CM (6") TO ALLOW FOR HEM AND HEADING.

2. MEASURING CURTAIN WIDTH

(D) MEASURE ACROSS THE WINDOW, BETWEEN THE ARCHITRAVES.

(E) ADD AN EXTRA 30CM (12") ON EACH SIDE TO ALLOW FOR STACK BACKS

REMEMBER TO ADD SEAM ALLOWANCES.

3. MEASURING UP FOR BLINDS

(F) BLINDS SHOULD BE FIXED 20CM (8") ABOVE THE ARCHITRAVE IF POSSIBLE TO MAXIMISE THE AMOUNT OF LIGHT INTO THE ROOM. MEASURE THE LENGTH OF THE WINDOW FROM THE ARCHITRAVE AT TOP TO THE SILL.

— NOW ADD 20CM (8") PLUS 3CM (1") AND YOUR USUAL SEAM ALLOWANCES.

(G) MEASURE THE WIDTH BETWEEN THE ARCHITRAVES ADD ON 5CM (2") TO EACH SIDE.

4. MEASURING UP FOR CURTAINS & BLINDS IN A RECESSED WINDOW

(H) MEASURE THE LENGTH FROM TOP TO BOTTOM OF THE RECESS — MEASURE THE WIDTH OF RECESS AND ADD SEAM ALLOWANCES. ALWAYS MEASURE FOR A BLIND IN THE MIDDLE, TOP AND BOTTOM AS WINDOWS CAN BE IRREGULARLY SHAPED.

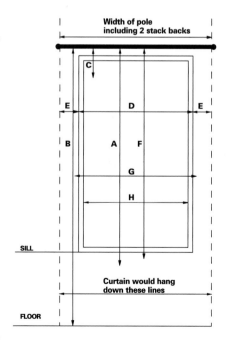

Width of pole
including 2 stack backs

C

E   D   E

B   A   F

G

H

SILL

Curtain would hang
down these lines

FLOOR

Fabric Needs

PLANNING AHEAD

YOU NEED TO MAKE SOME IMPORTANT DECISIONS AT THIS POINT.

1. DECIDE THE TYPE OF CURTAIN OR BLIND TREATMENT YOU WANT.

2. IF CURTAINS - WHICH HEADING? WHICH POLE, TRACK OR PELMET?

3. IF CURTAINS - WHAT LENGTH? - LONG OR SHORT?

4. IF A BLIND - WILL IT BE INSIDE RECESS OR OUTSIDE?

5. CHECK WHICH WAY WINDOWS OPEN SO YOUR CURTAIN OR BLIND WILL CLEAR WHEN WINDOW OPEN.

6. CHECK THERE IS ROOM EITHER SIDE OF WINDOW TO ALLOW STACK BACK SO LIGHT IS ALLOWED INTO ROOM.

7. MAKE SURE THERE IS ENOUGH ROOM ABOVE WINDOW SO YOU CAN PUT A FIXING UP. IF NOT YOU WILL HAVE TO HANG FROM THE CEILING FINDING RAFTERS FOR SOUND FIXING OR INSIDE RECESS. .

AFTER MEASURING UP (SEE PAGE 9)

LOOK AT YOUR DRAWING WITH THE MEASUREMENTS AND FOLLOW THIS ROUGH GUIDE. (IT'S ROUGH BECAUSE EVERYONE HAS THEIR OWN IDEAS OF HOW THEY WANT THEIR WINDOW COVERINGS TO LOOK).

1. TAKE THE LENGTH OF CURTAIN + 3 TIMES WIDTH OF POLE FOR VOILES/SHEERS

$2\frac{1}{2}$	"	FORMAL CURTAINS
$2\frac{1}{2}$	"	UNLINED CURTAINS
$1\frac{1}{2}$	"	CONTEMPORARY STYLES
1	"	PANELS

2. ADD 7CM (3") FOR HEADING + 15CM (6") FOR HEM ON EACH LENGTH DROP.

3. ADD 6CMS (2½") FOR EACH SEAM ON WIDTH OF CURTAIN.

CALCULATING FABRIC FOR BLINDS

TAKE THE LENGTH OF BLIND PLUS 20CM (8") EXTRA FABRIC TO WRAP OVER THE TOP AND BOTTOM BATTENS. IF YOU ARE COVERING PELMET BOARD YOU NEED EXTRA FABRIC. YOU ONLY NEED TO ALLOW FOR PATTERN REPEAT IF YOU ARE JOINING WIDTHS OR IF YOU WANT PATTERN IN THE CENTRE OF THE BLIND.

CALCULATING LINING QUANTITIES

THE LINING REQUIRED ON LINED CURTAIN IS CUT SMALLER THAN THE FABRIC. THEREFORE DO NOT ADD ANY ALLOWANCES FOR SEAMS ONLY ALLOW 10CM (4") FOR HEM. I DO LIKE TO ADD A TINY BIT HERE AND THERE AS YOU CAN ALWAYS CUT AWAY ANY EXCESS FABRIC BUT YOU CAN'T ADD IT ON!

Essential ingredients

Sewing machine

Dressmaker's scissors

Pinking sheers

Embroidery scissors

Tape measure (Cloth & metal)

Tailor's chalk

Pins with coloured heads

Sewing needles (all sizes)

Thimble

Unpicker

Cottons

Hem weights

Touch & close tape (Velcro)

An eyelet hole kit

Tracing paper (I use parchment cooking paper)

Steam iron

Stitches

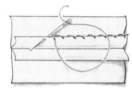

Overlocking Stitch
Used to stop fabric fraying on hand sewn curtains

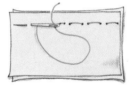

Running, gathering & Basting Stitch
Stitch used for basting or gathering

Blanket Stitch
Use thick wool or Thread

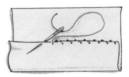

Hemming stitch used to hem and to stop fraying

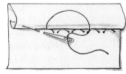

Loose stitch
Sometimes used to loosely attach lining to fabric

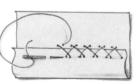

Herringbone stitch
Used for hems or to neaten seams

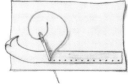

Blind stitching
When sewing on Ribbons and braids by hand

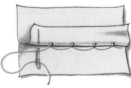

Locking stitch
Used for joining interlining to the main fabric

PREPARATION:
TAKE TIME TO CHECK YOU HAVE EVERYTHING YOU NEED BEFORE MAKING A START. CHECK OUT YOUR BASIC INGREDIENTS AS WELL AS YOUR SHOPPING LIST

TIP: DOUBLE CHECK THAT YOU REMEMBERED TO ALLOW ENOUGH FABRIC FOR PATTERN REPEATS BEFORE CUTTING — SEE MEASURING SECTION.

A. CUTTING OUT — CUT FABRIC ON LONG CLEAN SURFACE. CHECK FABRIC IS RUNNING THE RIGHT WAY. AND USE A SET SQUARE AND METAL RULER TO MARK A STRAIGHT LINE ACROSS THE FABRIC. MEASURE 1ST DROP DOWN SELVAGE LINE AND MARK YOUR TOP AND BOTTOM WITH PINS MAKING SURE YOUR NEXT DROP MATCHES AS (B). CONTINUE THIS WAY FOR REST OF WIDTHS — WIDTHS GO ON OUTER EDGES. PIN AND BASTE AS C

B. PATTERN MATCH. PUT THE TWO SELVEDGES TOGETHER AND LINE UP PRINT FACING YOU ON BOTH SIDES AS IN THE DIAGRAM — POP A PIN IN AT THE TOP AND BOTTOM TO HOLD IN PLACE AS A MARKER.

C. PIN AND SEW — LAY YOUR 2 CURTAIN LENGTHS DOWN ON YOUR SEWING TABLE FACE TO FACE — SELVEDGE TO SELVEDGE. PLACE THE PINS HORIZONTALLY AS IN THE DIAGRAM. ALLOW 2CM (1") FROM SELVEGE FOR SEWING LINE. THIS IS FOR A PLAIN FABRIC, IF IT IS A PRINT THEN THE SEWING LINE DEPENDS ON THE PATTERN MATCH. MACHINE STRAIGHT OVER GAP IN PINS, DON'T WORRY THEY WON'T BREAK NOR WILL YOUR MACHINE NEEDLE VERY CLEVER! IF YOU DON'T BELIEVE IT YOU CAN USE A RUNNING STITCH INSTEAD.

D. SNIP SEAMS — GO QUITE CLOSE TO MACHINE LINE — SNIPPING STOPS ANY PUCKERING OR GATHERING ON SEAMS — ESSENTIAL WHEN MACHINING SHAPED PARTS OF A CURTAIN. PRESS SEAM OPEN WITH A FAIRLY HOT IRON.

TIP: USE A LARGE STITCH WHEN SEWING SEAMS AS A SMALL TIGHT SEAM CAUSES PULLING AND PUCKERING AND DOESN'T ALWAYS PRESS OUT.

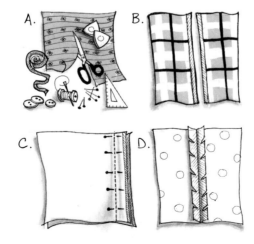

PREPARATION
- CUT OUT YOUR FABRIC AS PAGE 12 – REMEMBER TO ADD SEAM ALLOWANCES FOR HEM, HEADINGS AND SIDESEAMS

- JOIN YOUR WIDTHS TOGETHER – PIN, BASTE + MACHINE TOGETHER

- OVERLOCK ALL SEAMS – PRESS OPEN

MAKING A START!
1. ON THE LEADING AND BACK EDGES, TURN THE EDGES IN DOUBLE 3CM (1") – PIN + BASTE THESE WITHIN 7CM (2") FROM THE TOP OF THE CURTAINS AND 15CM (6") FROM THE BOTTOM

2. TURN THE HEM ALLOWANCE 15CM (6") DOUBLE AND PRESS. THEN OPEN OUT & PRESS IN THE 2 MITRES TO THE SEAM LINE

3. CUT AWAY ANY EXCESS FABRIC

4. FOLD BACK THE DOUBLE HEM, SLIP STITCH THE HEM

5. TURN OVER THE TOP TO PUT ON YOUR HEADING TAPE – DEPENDING ON WHAT KIND OF HEADING YOUR CURTAINS ARE HAVING

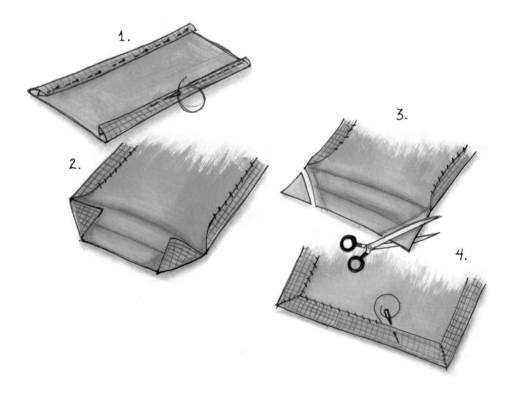

Lined Curtains

PREPARATIONS
- CUT OUT YOUR CURTAIN FABRIC AS ON PAGE 13

- CUT THE LINING THE SAME SIZE AS YOUR FINISHED CURTAIN (IN OTHER WORDS DO NOT ADD ANY SEAM ALLOWANCES!)

MAKING A START

1. TURN UP THE HEM ON THE LINING 3CM (1½") DOUBLE THEN MACHINE THE HEM AND PRESS.

2. PRESS UNDER THE RAW EDGES 2CM (1") ON THE SIDES AND TOP ONLY

3. PLACE THE LINING CENTRALLY ONTO THE CURTAIN WITH THE WRONG SIDES TOGETHER. PIN INTO POSITION AND THEN BASTE. FINALLY SLIP STITCH ALL AROUND EXCEPT FOR THE HEM

TIP – TO STOP THE LINING FLAPPING AROUND BEHIND THE CURTAIN YOU CAN ALWAYS PUT A LOOSE CHAIN STITCH HERE AND THERE

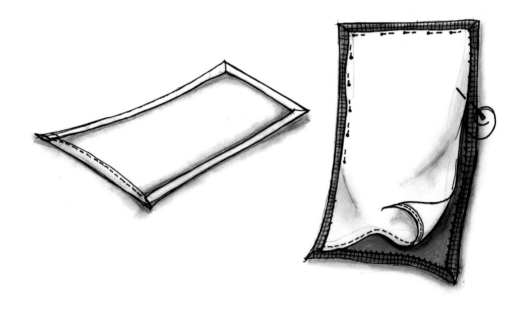

CHECK IT OUT:
FOR CLASSIC CURTAIN HEADINGS 1+2+3 YOU CAN BUY TAPE FROM YOUR HABERDASHERY STORE.

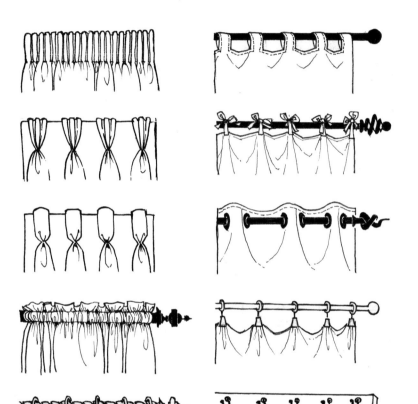

1. PENCIL PLEAT

2. TRIPLE PINCH PLEAT

3. GOBLET OR TULIP

4. SLOTTED HEADING OR ROD POCKET

5. SOFT PINCH PLEATS

6. TAB

7. TIES

8. EYELET

9. CLIP

10. LOOP

Classic Styles

Check it out:

Make sure you but the correct thickness of pole for your fabric. This is just a rough guide. Heavy fabric such as velvet, chenille and tweed use 6cm diameter (2"). Medium fabrics which are to be lined use 5cm (2"). Light voiles or cotton unlined, use 2.5cm diametre (1")

Preparation

A pole has to take a lot of weight in some cases and opening and closing your curtains can put strain on the fixing. Be careful when fixing the brackets to use long enough screws. Always follow the manufacturer's instructions.

Tip: Buy a plain untreated (unvarnished) wooden pole for painting.

 1. Ball

 2. Provencal style

 3. Reeded ball and pole

 4. Fluted ball

 5. Acorn

 6. Urn-decorative pole

 7. Trumpet-2 colours of wood

 8. Art deco

 9. Banded ball-fabric covered pole

 10. Inverted rib and ogee

 11. Style of early Victorian spinning top

 12. Leaf and acorn

 13. Minaret candy twist pole

 14. Victorian scroll

 15. Coronet-decorative pole

 16. Otterman

CHECK IT OUT
STAINLESS STEEL, IRON, ANTIQUED METAL. THERE ARE SO MANY TO CHOOSE FROM YOU ARE SPOILT FOR CHOICE. IF THE POLE IS LONGER THAN 3 METRES (10FT) YOU WILL NEED A CENTRE BRACKET.

TIP: BUY A GOOD QUALITY METAL POLE THEN IT WON'T RUST OTHERWISE VARNISH A CHEAPER ONE WITH A YACHT VARNISH TO STOP IT RUSTING.

 1. STEEL SPIRE

 9. ROPED BALL

 2. WOODEN 'BAMBOO' BALL

 10. ROPED CONE

 3. STEEL RIBBON BALL

 11. STEEL TRUMPET

 4. IRON BUTTON

 12 STEEL CORKSCREW

 5. IRON BALL

 13 STEEL RIB

 6. IRON KNOT

 14 METAL BALL

 7. CAGE AND BALL

 15. STEEL SPOTTED BALL

 8. SHEPHERDS CROOK

16. THREE TONE CONE BALLS

CHECK IT OUT
TENSION WIRE TRACKING CAN ONLY SUPPORT LIGHTWEIGHT FABRICS
SUCH AS VOILES (SHEERS) OR LINENS – DON'T LINE.

WIRE TRACKING GOES FROM WALL TO WALL – OBVIOUSLY WITHIN REASON
– OR SIDE TO SIDE IN A WINDOW RECESS. (SEE DIAGRAM 3)

TIP: READ THE MANUFACTURERS INSTRUCTIONS CAREFULLY OTHERWISE IT
CAN BE A NIGHTMARE

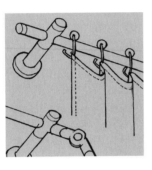

1. STAINLESS STEEL
ROLLER LINE POLE.
CAN ALSO BE
USED FOR ANGLES

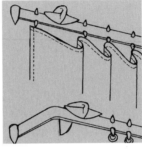

2. STAINLESS STEEL
FLAT POLE FOR
BAY WINDOW

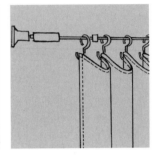

3. TENSION WIRE
SYSTEM USED FROM
WALL TO WALL

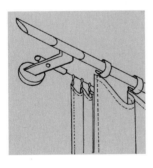

4. STAINLESS STEEL
POLE CAN BE USED
WITH TENSION
WIRE FOR SECOND
CURTAIN

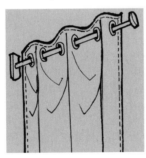

5. POLE USED TO
DRESS WINDOW
OR AS A ROOM
DIVIDER

6. VARIOUS METAL
SPIRAL RINGS ARE
GREAT FUN-USE
WITH EYELET HOLES

CHECK IT OUT:
I PREFER CURTAINS THAT HANG STRAIGHT AND ONE'S THAT CRUMPLE ON THE FLOOR BUT THERE ARE TIMES WHEN YOU NEED TO HAVE TIE-BACKS TO MAXIMISE THE AMOUNT OF LIGHT COMING INTO THE ROOM OR PERHAPS, IF YOUR CURTAINS ARE IN A FORMAL SETTING THEN A PAIR OF TASSEL TIE-BACKS WILL COMPLETE THE ROOM IN STYLE.

CHEAT: TRY PLATTING STRING OR ROPE TOGETHER AND ADD IVY OR LAVENDER TO THE END THEN TIE A LARGE KNOT.

TIP: FIND YOUR LOCAL FORGER FROM AN INTERIORS MAGAZINE AND DESIGN YOUR OWN "EMBRACES" MAYBE WITH YOUR INITIALS?

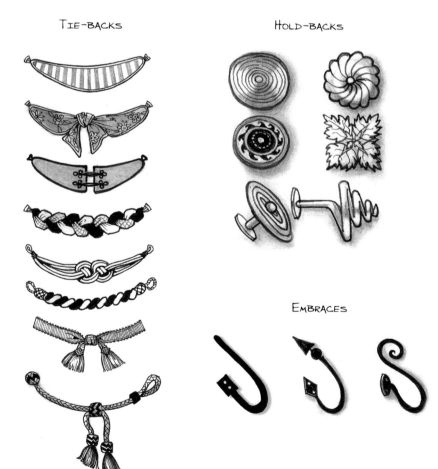

TIE-BACKS

HOLD-BACKS

EMBRACES

Ribbons + Beads

TAKE A SIMPLE CURTAIN DESIGN, AN ORDINARY PIECE OF FABRIC, PUT THEM TOGETHER, ADD A WELL CHOSEN TRIMMING AND THE WHOLE EFFECT CAN BE ABSOLUTELY STUNNING. YOU CAN USE LOADS OF BEADS, BRAIDS AND FRINGING – MIX THEM ALTOGETHER – OR JUST USE A SIMPLE ROW OF BEADS – BELIEVE ME IT WILL TRANSFORM YOUR CURTAINS.

 1. GIMP

 2. PICOT RIBBON

 3. ROPE

 4. FLANGED ROPE

5. SLOTTED HEADED FRINGE

 6. LOOP FRINGE

 7. FAN EDGE

 8. BOBBLE FRINGE

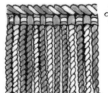 9. BULLION FRINGE

 10. CRYSTAL SATIN RIBBON

 11. BEAD FRINGE

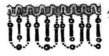 12. LOOPED BEADS ON GIMP

 13. STRINGS OF BEADS

 14. ASSORTED CRYSTAL BEADS ON SATIN RIBBON

  15. CUT FRINGE WITH BEADED HANGERS

Fringes + Tassels

SIMPLE AND DELICIOUS—
USE ANY WAY YOU WANT

JANE CHURCHILL
LARKFIELD RANGE

Braids + Beads

ELABORATE BRAIDS AND FROSTED BEADS
ADD THESE LUXURIOUS GOLD BRAIDS AND OPULENT FROSTED BEADS TO
CHENILLE, BROCADES OR EVEN A SACKING CLOTH AND YOUR CURTAINS
WILL LOOK A MILLION DOLLARS

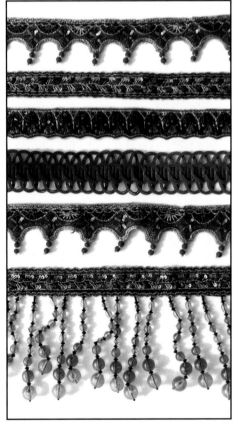

WENDY CUSHING'S
RUBARIS RANGE

WONDERFUL TASSELS – LOOK GOOD ENOUGH TO EAT.
ADD THEM TO BLINDS, CUSHIONS ETC AS TIE BACKS OR SIMPLY
HAVE THEM HANGING ABOUT...

1. FEATHER TASSELS
2. KEY TASSELS
3. LEATHER BUTTON
4. OCTAGONAL DOUBLE TASSELS

THE CLASSICS

BEADED TASSELS

KEY TASSELS

SLIM CONTEMPORARY TASSELS

Floral Fabrics

1. FLORALS
2. NATURAL WEAVES
3. EARTHY COLOURS
4. CHECKS + STRIPES
5. SILKS
6. VOILES (SHEERS) & LACE

FABRIC DATA:
COTTON FABRICS ARE ALWAYS POPULAR AS THEY ARE EASY TO WORK WITH AS WELL AS BEING RELATIVELY INEXPENSIVE AND HARDWEARING. SMALL FLORAL PRINTS GO WELL IN A COTTAGE OR IN A CHILD'S ROOM WHEREAS LARGER PRINTS WORK BETTER IN ROOMS WITH TALL CEILINGS AND BIG WINDOWS.

TIP: TAKE CARE TO PATTERN MATCH YOUR FABRIC (SEE PAGE 12)

1. JANE CHURCHILL
   SYLVAN CHECK

2. CATH KIDSTON
   SCATTERED FLOWERS

3. JANE CHURCHILL
   RAMBLING ROSE

4. ANNA FRENCH
   RUSJA

5. JANE CHURCHILL
   TRELLIS TOILE

6. CATH KIDSTON
   ROSE PAISLEY

7. ANNE FRENCH
   JAPONICA

8. CATH KIDSTON
   ROSE STRIPE

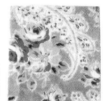

FABRIC DATA:

NATURAL FABRICS IN NEUTRAL COLOURS IS IN MY OPINION A WINNING COMBINATION — YOU CAN'T GO WRONG! YOU CAN LEAVE THIS FABRIC UNLINED AS IT THEN FALLS WELL AND DOESN'T LOSE THAT NATURAL LOOK. LINEN IS THE MOST VERSATILE OF FABRICS LINED UNLINED, TRIMMED OR UNTRIMMED — IT CAN LOOK CRISP OR CRUMPLED, WHATEVER YOU WISH.

TIP: I USE UNBLEACHED CALICO WITH INSETS OF COTTON LACE — UNLINED IT LOOKS WONDERFUL AND COSTS "ALMOST NOTHING".

ANOTHER TIP: USE LINING (IT COMES IN COLOURS TOO) FOR CURTAINS IF YOU ARE ON A REALLY LOW BUDGET — PUT LOTS OF RIC-RAC OR TRIMMING ON THEM AND NO ONE WILL EVER KNOW!

Natural Weaves

1. MALABAR
   NSIL 24

2. MALABAR
   NJUT 05

3. MALABAR
   HERRINGBONE

4. MALABAR
   NSIL 08

5. SHEILA COOMBS
   INDIAN SUMMER
   RAJPUT 02

6. SCHUMACHER
   GWENTH LINEN

7. ANNA FRENCH
   WILLIAM 67

8. MALABAR
   NS 1211

Earthy Weaves + Colours

FABRIC DATA:

RUSTIC FABRICS CHUNKY WEAVES IN EARTHY COLOURS —
GALLOWAY PLAIDS & HARRIS TWEEDS — A TRUE COUNTRY
ORGANIC FEEL. THESE FABRICS BLEND IN ANYWHERE AND
GIVE OUT A FABULOUS CUDDLY FEEL. THEY DON'T NEED TO
BE LINED BUT IF LINED, THEY ARE IN MY MIND EVEN
MORE COMFORTABLE TO LIVE WITH.

1. OSBORNE & LITTLE
   FEZ

2. SHELIA COOMBS
   RAJPUT

3. ANNA FRENCH
   BIRD IN THE BUSH

4. BEACON HILL
   SQUARED OFF

5. MALABAR
   TANTRA

6. BEACON HILL
   LINEN HERRINGBONE

7. OSBORNE & LITTLE
   FEZ

8. COLEFAX & FOWLER
   GALLOWAY PLAID

FABRIC DATA:
THE WONDERFUL THING ABOUT COTTON IS THAT IT'S INEXPENSIVE
(GENERALLY), IT'S READILY AVAILABLE AND COMES IN BRILLIANT
COLOURS, WASHES WELL, MACHINES WELL — WHAT MORE CAN I SAY!
IT'S NOT ABSOLUTELY NECESSARY TO LINE COTTON CURTAINS,
SOMEHOW THEY ALWAYS LOOK GOOD.

BELOW I'VE MIXED CHECKS + STRIPED COTTONS IN WITH EMBROIDERED
COTTONS WHICH IS FUN — USE THE CHECKS AS CUSHIONS MAYBE MIX
THEM ALL UP, IT LOOKS GREAT.

1. MALABAR
   JANE CHURCHILL
   DESIGNERS GUILD
   JANE CHURCHILL

2. DESIGNERS GUILD
   DESIGNERS GUILD
   SCHUMACHER

3. DESIGNERS GUILD
   DESIGNERS GUILD
   SCHUMACHER

4. CATH KIDSTON
   CATH KIDSTON
   DESIGNERS GUILD
   CATH KIDSTON

GROSGRAIN RIBBON WITH SADDLE
STITCHING FROM V.V. ROULEAUX

Woven Silks

FABRIC DATA:

SILK IS ONE OF THE MOST GORGEOUS FABRICS ON THE MARKET – IT'S LUXURIOUS YET NOW AFFORDABLE. USE PLAIN WOVEN SILK FOR MOST DESIGNS OF CURTAINS AND YOU WON'T BE DISAPPOINTED, THEY ALWAYS LOOK STUNNING. THERE ARE A NUMBER OF PRETTY EMBROIDERED SILKS WHICH LOOK SOFT AND GENTLE FOR YOUR BEDROOM CURTAINS.

TIP: WHEN SEWING SILK FABRICS BE SURE YOUR NEEDLE IS VERY FINE. PUT IN A NEW ONE AS SILK HAS A TENDENCY TO SNAG.

1. JANE CHURCHILL
   MARISA

2. MALABAR INDIAN
   SILK
   KENKA

3. MALABAR INDIAN
   SILK
   KENKA

4. DESIGNERS GUILD
   LUCIA

5. DESIGNERS GUILD
   LUCIA

6. MALABAR INDIAN
   SILK
   KENKA

7. MALABAR INDIAN
   SILK
   KENKA

8. MALABAR INDIAN
   SILK
   KALIFA 02

Voiles (Sheers) + Laces

FABRIC DATA:

MOST HOUSES HAVE AT LEAST ONE PAIR OF VOILE OR LACE CURTAIN HANGING AT THEIR WINDOWS NOWADAYS USE PLENTY OF FABRIC, DON'T CUT ANY CORNERS, AND AS YOU DON'T HAVE TO LINE THEM YOU CAN SPEND MORE MONEY ON YOUR FABRIC.

WONDERFUL FLOATY SILK VOILES, EMBROIDERED SILK ORGANZA'S FROM INDIA AND MADRAS COTTON LACE, PUT THEM INTO ANY ROOM SETTING AND YOU WILL ALWAYS BE PLEASED WITH THE RESULT.

1. JANE CHURCHILL
   FLORIAN SHEER

2. JANE CHURCHILL
   MARISA SHEER

3. GREEF
   CHRISTINA SHEER

4. SCHUMACHER
   MUGUET DES BOIS

5. SCHUMACHER
   GENEVIEVE MADRAS

6. MALABAR
   CHECK SHEER

7. JANE CHURCHILL
   ROSMAR SHEER

8. ANNE FRENCH
   EDWARDIAN LEAVES
   MADRAS

Pencil Pleated Heading

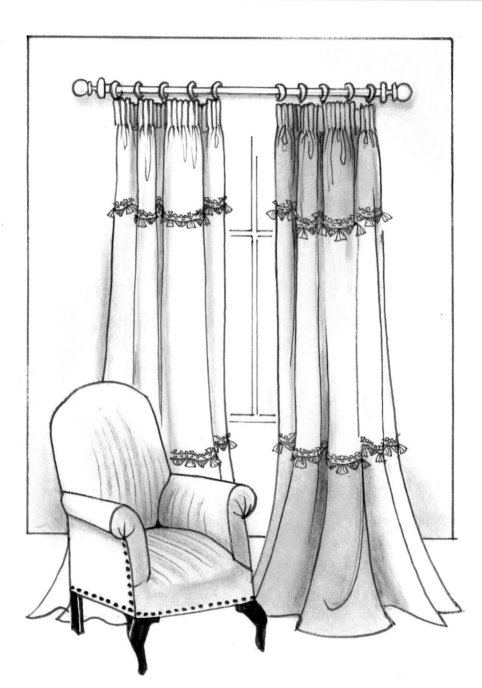

PLAIN AND SIMPLE JUST A TOUCH OF TASSEL
FRINGE TO COMPLETE THE PICTURE

ESSENTIAL INGREDIENTS

MAIN FABRIC

CONTRAST FABRIC

TASSEL FRINGING

HEADING TAPE (PENCIL PLEAT)

CURTAIN HOOKS

PREPARATION

- WHEN YOU HAVE MEASURED YOUR WINDOWS AND WORKED OUT YOUR FABRIC NEEDS YOU NEED TO ADD YOUR USUAL SEAM ALLOWANCES BUT ADD 2 EXTRA ONES IN THE LENGTH FOR THE CUT THROUGHS

- CUT YOUR TRIM TO THE WIDTH OF YOUR CURTAINS PLUS EXTRA FOR TURNINGS. YOU NEED 2/3 IN THE MAIN COLOUR AND 1/3 IN CONTRAST COLOUR

MAKING A START

1. SEW YOUR PIECES TOGETHER (DIAGRAM 1). PRESS THE SEAMS FLAT ê APPLY THE TRIMMING OVER THE SEAMS. NOW MAKE UP THE REST OF YOUR CURTAINS AS LINED CURTAINS PAGE 14 – LEAVING THE TOP OF CURTAINS READY TO APPLY YOUR HEADING TAPE

2. AT THE TOP OF THE CURTAINS TURN DOWN AN 8CM (3") FOLD TO THE WRONG SIDE. PRESS. POSITION YOUR HEADING TAPE ALONG THE TOP EDGE ABOUT 1CM (½") DOWN. TUCK UNDER THE RAW EDGES OF THE TAPE AT BOTH ENDS. PIN AND BASTE TOP ê BOTTOM OF YOUR TAPE. MACHINE. DO NOT FORGET TO TIE A KNOT IN THE TWO STRINGS AT THE LEADING EDGE BEFORE YOU PULL THEM TO FORM YOU PLEATS. PULL THE CORDS UNTIL YOU GET TO THE RIGHT WIDTH FOR YOUR WINDOWS AND SECURE STRINGS WITH A BOW. PUT YOUR HOOKS INTO HEADING, EVENLY DEPENDING HOW MANY RINGS YOU HAVE

TIP: IF YOU BUY MULTI POCKET HEADING TAPE YOU CAN PUT YOUR HOOKS IN AT VARIOUS POSITIONS WHICH CAN HELP IF THE FLOOR IS UNEVEN

1.

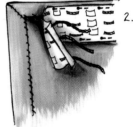

2.

ADDING A WIDE CONTRAST
BOARDER LIKE THIS CAN
TRANSFORM A BASIC PAIR
OF CURTAINS

ESSENTIAL INGREDIENTS

FABRIC

CONTRAST FABRIC

PENCIL PLEATED HEADING TAPE

LINING

WEIGHTS (COIN TYPE)

PREPARATION

- FIX YOUR POLE INTO POSITION AND CHECK YOUR MEASUREMENTS AGAIN.

- CUT OUT YOUR MAIN FABRIC FOR THE CURTAINS AS WELL AS THE LINING — NOT FORGETTING THE USUAL SEAM ALLOWANCES..

- CUT OUT YOUR CONTRAST BORDERS — YOU NEED 2 X YOUR LENGTH + SEAM ALLOWANCES AND 2 X HOW EVER MANY WIDTHS YOUR CURTAINS ARE — THE CORNERS ON THE LEADING EDGE MUST BE CUT AT A 45 DEGREE ANGLE AS DIAGRAM.

MAKING A START

1. SEW YOUR PIECES OF BORDER TOGETHER AT A 45 DEGREE ANGLE AND PRESS SEAMS OPEN.

1.

2. LAY THE INSIDE EDGE OF THE BORDER TO THE OUTSIDE OF THE EDGE OF THE CURTAINS WITH THE RIGHT SIDES TOGETHER. PIN, BASTE AND MACHINE THE EDGES TOGETHER.

2.

3. THEN MAKE UP YOUR CURTAINS AS ON PAGE 14 FOR LINED CURTAINS.

4. FINALLY PUT YOUR HEADING TAPE ON ABOUT 2½CM (1") FROM THE TOP OF YOUR CURTAINS.

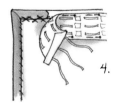
4.

Italian Stringing

ITALIAN STRINGING SWEEPS
THIS RICHLY COLOURED
CURTAIN TO ONE SIDE

ESSENTIAL INGREDIENTS

POLE, RINGS AND BRACKETS

CORD, RINGS AND CLEAT

PENCIL PLEATED HEADING TAPE

MAIN FABRIC

CONTRAST FABRIC

TRIMMING

TIP: DON'T USE A VERY HEAVY FABRIC AS THE STRINGING IS NOT THAT STRONG

PREPARATION

- PUT UP YOUR POLE AND FIX THE CLEAT ABOUT 1/3 UP FROM THE FLOOR

- CUT THE TOP AND CONTRAST FABRICS THE SAME SIZE WITH USUAL TOP, HEM + SIDE SEAM ALLOWANCES

MAKING A START

1. LAY THE BROCADE AND THE CONTRAST FACE TO FACE (RIGHT SIDES TOGETHER). PIN, BASTE AND THEN MACHINE TOGETHER LEAVING THE TOP OPEN — TURN THROUGH TO FORM A 'BAG' AND PRESS SEAMS.

2. APPLY THE HEADING TAPE — FOLD DOWN THE TOPS OF THE CURTAIN INTO THE BAG ABOUT 3CM (1"). CHECK YOUR CURTAIN LENGTH AND IF TOO LONG YOU COULD PUT A BIGGER TUCK IN — PIN THE HEADING TAPE 1CM (½") FROM THE TOP. BASTE AND THEN MACHINE. TIE A KNOT IN THE STRINGS OF THE TAPE AND PULL INTO PLEATS TO REQUIRED WIDTH, THEN TIE A BOW WITH THE LONG STRINGS. MAKE SURE PLEATS ARE EVEN.

3. SEW BRAID ONTO LEADING EDGE

4. PLACE THE CURTAIN RIGHT SIDE DOWN. SEW A CORDING RING ON THE CONTRAST FABRIC AT THE LEADING EDGE, ABOUT 1/3 OF THE WAY DOWN THE CURTAIN. SEW ANOTHER 4 OR 5 RINGS AT A 45 DEGREE ANGLE TOWARDS THE OTHER EDGE OF THE CURTAIN ABOUT 20CM (8") APART. KNOT THE CORD ONTO THE FIRST RING AND THREAD THROUGH THE OTHER RINGS — LEAVE PLENTY OF CORD AT THE END TO SECURE INTO A CLEAT ON THE WALL LIKE A ROMAN BLIND.

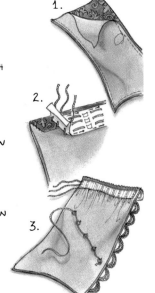

1.

2.

3.

Pencil Pleated Heading

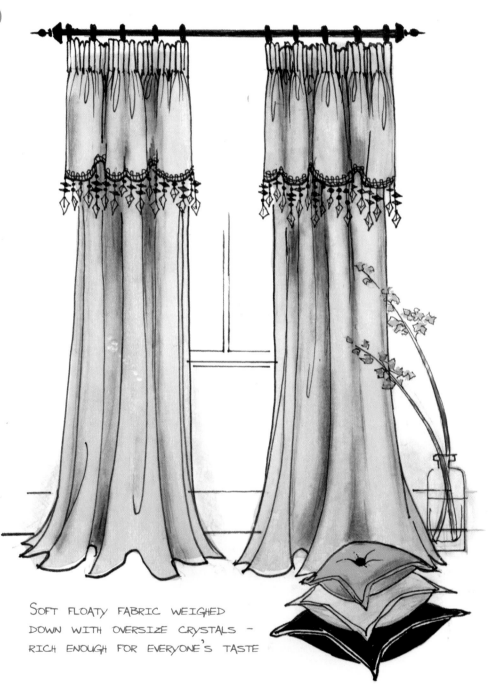

SOFT FLOATY FABRIC WEIGHED
DOWN WITH OVERSIZE CRYSTALS —
RICH ENOUGH FOR EVERYONE'S TASTE

Essential Ingredients
Silk fabric – or similar

Lining

Pencil pleat heading tape

Trimming with crystals

Extra crystals if needed

Weights

Preparation
- When cutting, the standard length of the 'skirt' should be about 1/3 of the overall length of curtain. Cut heading tape and trimming to width of both curtains plus extra for turnings

- Make up curtains & 'skirts' as for lined curtains, see page 14, but leave the tops open

Making a Start
1. Put your 2 pieces together (curtain and 'skirt') face up and raw edges together at the top. Turn over the usual amount, pin, baste and lastly herringbone neatly as diagram 1

2. Place your heading tape 5cm (2") down from the top – pin, baste & machine top and bottom of the tape straight through as diagram 2

3. Hand sew on the trimming by using a back stitch – you can add extra crystals now if you wish

4. Tie a knot in the tape at the leading edge then pulling the 2 strings gather the heading to your required measurement making sure the pleats are even

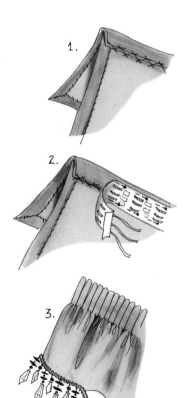

1.

2.

3.

Goblet Heading

TO ACHIEVE THIS TOTALLY PROFESSIONAL LOOK — ADD A
FEW INTERESTING TOUCHES HERE AND THERE

ESSENTIAL INGREDIENTS
POLE AND BRACKETS

FABRIC

LINING

BUCKRAM & WADDING OR COTTON WOOL

FLANGED ROPE (SEE GLOSSARY)

PREPARATION

- PUT UP YOUR POLE — CHECK MEASUREMENTS

- CUT YOUR CURTAINS OUT — THE WIDTH SHOULD BE 2.5 TIMES YOUR PELMET BOARD WIDTH — PLUS THE WIDTH OF THE 2 RETURNS.

- CUT 2 STRIPS OF BUCKRAM 10CM (4") WIDE BY THE WIDTH OF THE CURTAINS.

MAKING A START

1. LAY THE FABRIC RIGHT SIDE UP AND STITCH FLANGED ROPE TRIM AROUND THE EDGE (SEE DIAGRAM). LAY THE LINING ON TOP RIGHT SIDE DOWN — BASTE AROUND 3 EDGES MAKING SURE THAT THE FLANGE (FLAT PART) OF THE ROPE IS SYMMETRICAL BETWEEN THE 2 PIECES OF FABRIC. DON'T SEW RIGHT UP TO THE TOP — LEAVE ABOUT 25CM (10") LOOSE EITHER SIDE. TURN THROUGH TO FORM YOUR BAG AND PRESS FLAT.

2. PRESS OVER THE TOP 10CM (4") THEN OPEN UP AND LAY A PIECE OF BUCKRAM NEXT TO THE FOLD LINE AND HERRINGBONE ALL AROUND. FOLD THE TOP OVER TO COVER THE BUCKRAM AND HERRINGBONE (SEE DIAGRAM). THEN COMPLETE BY SEWING THE LINING IN PLACE.

3. TO WORK OUT HOW MANY GOBLETS YOU NEED, ALLOW ABOUT 15CM (6") FOR EACH GOBLET AND THE SAME FOR EACH GAP. THEN WITH THE RIGHT SIDE OF THE FABRIC FACING YOU, FOLD OVER YOUR 15CM PLEAT — BASTE & MACHINE AS DIAGRAM TO JUST BELOW BUCKRAM.

4. SECURE BASE OF EACH GOBLET WITH A FEW STITCHES — OPEN UP THE GOBLETS AND STUFF WITH WADDING.

5. MAKE BUTTONS. CUT SQUARES OF BUCKRAM OR CARDBOARD AND CUT LARGER SQUARE IN FABRIC — GLUE INTO PLACE AND SNIP OFF CORNERS AND GLUE SMALLER SQUARE OF LINING TO COVER.

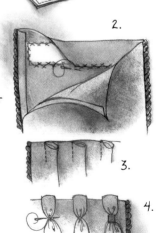

1.

2.

3.

4.

With a Valance

TRY USING A FLAMBOYANT FABRIC
ON THIS VERY CLASSICAL STYLE

Essential Ingredients

Fabric

Pencil pleat heading tape (for curtains)

Lining

Tie back and hooks

Buckram

Pelmet board and brackets

Fan edged trimming and rope

Tracking for curtains

Touch-and-close tape

Staple gun

Preparation

- Cover the pelmet board – put into place together with curtain track
- Staple 1st side of touch-and-close tape to front of pelmet
- Cut the main curtain fabric to your measurements and make up as page 14 (lined curtains) – put on heading tape as page 34 – press then put on your curtain hooks and hang.

Tip: Before you continue go to page 124 where you will find some Templates. When you have studied these – proceed!

A. Measure the actual width of the pelmet board plus the returns (sides) and cut a template (use newspaper?) to this width and, as a guide cut the longest length about $\frac{1}{4}$ of the length of your main curtains – fold over the paper template to find your centre line and shape the bottom edge with a dotted line. Blue tack your template to the pelmet and check the proportions – adjust accordingly.

B. To cut the 2nd elongated template, simply multiply the 1st width by 2.5 and add on the returns. Now take the centre measurement off the original template and transfer to the elongated one, do the same at both ends and continue to take measurements at regular intervals, say every 10cm (4") then all you need to do is join up the dots and you have a shaped valance, well nearly!

Making a Start

1. Join together your valance pieces and do the same with the lining – press.

2. Pin your finished template on to your fabric and remembering to add your seam allowances top and bottom, make a dotted line around the shape – cut it out – then repeat for lining. Make up the valance and lining as for lined curtains (see page 14)

3. Now go to page 39 – follow instructions 2 and 3 to make the goblets.

4. Sew on the fan edge trim and knot and loop the rope at the base of the goblets – stitch the other side of the touch and close tape to the back of the fabric about 2cm (1") from the top and press valance into place.

With a Valance

LOOKS EXPENSIVE AND I EXPECT USING A FABRIC LIKE
THIS IT WILL BE! BUT IT'S WORTH EVERY PENNY.

ESSENTIAL INGREDIENTS

FABRIC

LINING

BULLION FRINGE

PENCIL PLEATED HEADING TAPE (CURTAINS)

PENCIL PLEATED HEADING TAPE
(WITH TOUCH-AND-CLOSE BACKING FOR VALANCE)

TASSEL TIE-BACKS AND HOOKS

PELMET BOARD AND BRACKETS

PREPARATION
- COVER THE PELMET BOARD WITH FABRIC AND PUT INTO POSITION ALONG WITH CURTAIN TRACK.

- CUT OUT AND MAKE UP YOUR BASIC LINED CURTAINS - (SEE PAGE 14). PRESS AND HANG IN PLACE.

TIP: BEFORE YOU GO ANY FURTHER GO TO PAGE 124 WHERE YOU WILL FIND SOME TEMPLATES FOR THIS DESIGN - THEY SHOULD HELP!

MAKING A START
1. GO TO PAGE 41 AND FOLLOW INSTRUCTIONS A & B

2. FOLLOW INSTRUCTIONS 1 & 2 ON PAGE 41

3. PUT THE HEADING TAPE (THE ONE WITH THE TOUCH-AND-CLOSE TAPE INCORPORATED) ON TO THE BACK OF THE VALANCE ABOUT 2CM (1") FROM THE TOP - PIN BASTE AND THEN SEW ALL AROUND. KNOT THE STRINGS TOGETHER ON THE LEADING EDGE AND PULL GENTLY TO FORM THE PENCIL PLEATS UNTIL IT IS CORRECT WIDTH - MAKE SURE THAT THE PLEATS ARE EVEN, IE A BOW WITH THE STRINGS AND PUSH IT INTO THE POCKET OF THE TAPE.

4. AT THIS STAGE YOU CAN SEW ON YOUR BULLION FRINGE EITHER ON THE HEM OR SET INTO THE FABRIC. FINALLY PRESS THE VALANCE INTO PLACE ONTO THE PELMET BOARD.

Pinch Pleated Heading

LOOP BACK YOUR CURTAINS SO YOU GET A CHANCE TO ADMIRE THE CONTRAST FABRIC

Essential ingredients

Pole & brackets

2 tie backs, hooks & 2 rings

Fabric & contrast fabric (equal amounts)

Pinch pleated heading tape

Tip Make sure the pole is unvarnished as well as the rings — to paint them hang the pole by 2 pieces of string & the rings must hang from the metal hole. Undercoat 1st and then top coat

Preparation
- When you have worked out your fabric needs (page 10) cut out your 2 fabrics the same size

- Paint your pole and leave for 2 days before putting it up

Making a start

1. Put your 2 pieces of fabric face to face — pin, baste and machine around 3 sides — leaving the top open

2. Working from the back of the curtain turn the top over to the required length and place the heading tape 1cm (½") from the top edge. Pin & baste on the tape covering the raw edges — tuck under the edges at both ends

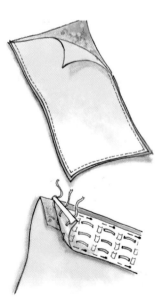

3. Finally machine the top and bottom of the tape. Tie a knot in the tape on the heading edge and pull the 2 strings to gather your heading to correct length. Make sure your pinch pleats are even and put a small stitch at the base to secure

4. Put a ring on the leading edge bottom corners & hang onto the curtain hooks

Pinch Pleated Heading

SIMPLICITY ITSELF

ESSENTIAL INGREDIENTS

FABRIC

LINING

BULLION FRINGE - WIDTH OF 2 CURTAINS & SEAM ALLOWANCES

SMALL TASSELS FOR HEADING - ONE ON EACH PLEAT

BUCKRAM

PREPARATION
- MAKE LINED CURTAINS AS PAGE 14 BUT LEAVE THE TOP OPEN
- CUT YOUR BUCKRAM THE SAME SIZE AS THE WIDTH OF BOTH CURTAINS

MAKING A START!
1. PRESS 10CM (4") OVER AT THE TOP
   OF THE CURTAIN - OPEN OUT AND
   PLACE THE BUCKRAM NEXT TO THE FOLD
   LINE, HERRINGBONE STITCH THE REMAINS
   OF THE LINING INTO POSITION

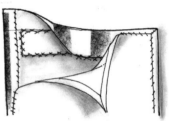

1.

2. WORK OUT HOW MANY PINCH PLEATS YOU
   NEED BY ALLOWING ABOUT 15CM (6") FOR
   EACH PLEAT AND THE SAME FOR THE GAPS.
   THEN WITH THE RIGHT SIDE OF THE
   FABRIC FACING YOU FOLD OVER YOUR
   15CM (6") PLEAT - BASTE AND MACHINE
   AS ILLUSTRATION JUST BELOW THE BUCKRAM

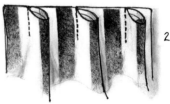

2.

3. SECURE THE TOP & THE BOTTOM OF
   YOUR PLEATS WITH A FEW STITCHES.
   SEE ILLUSTRATION

4. SEW ON THE TASSELS AT THE END OF EACH
   PLEAT AND SEW BULLION FRINGING ON THE
   HEM WRAPPING ANY SURPLUS OVER EDGES

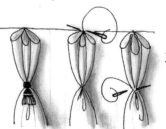

3.

Classic Curtains
Pocket Heading

Pocket Heading

THIS PROVENCAL FARMHOUSE STYLE IS EASY TO MAKE

Instructions

ESSENTIAL INGREDIENTS

MAIN CURTAIN FABRIC — VOILES (SHEERS) FOR CAFÉ CURTAINS

CURTAIN POLE AND BRACKETS

THIN ROD AND FITTINGS FOR RECESS WINDOW

RIBBONS

PREPARATION

- CUT OUT MAIN CURTAINS REMEMBERING THE USUAL SEAM ALLOWANCE PLUS AN EXTRA 2CM (1") DOUBLED FOR THE STAND ABOVE THE POLE & 10CM (4") FOR THE POCKET DEPENDING ON POLE SIZE

- CUT THE SHORT CAFÉ CURTAINS WITH THE SAME ALLOWANCES AT THE TOP & 3CM (1") FOR THE POCKET DEPENDING ALSO ON SIZE OF POLE

MAKING A START

1. AS THESE CURTAINS ARE UNLINED MAKE AS PAGE 13. OVERLOCK ALL RAW EDGES OR FRENCH SEAMS

2. HAVING MADE YOUR BASIC UNLINED CURTAINS TURN OVER THE TOPS OF EACH PAIR OF CURTAINS TO MAKE THE POCKET HEADINGS & SMALL STAND

3. FOR THE SHORT CAFÉ CURTAINS PIN THE 1ST ROW OF RIBBONS ON THE HEM THEN PIN ON THE NEXT 2 ROWS MAKING SURE THE DISTANCE BETWEEN EACH ROW IS EVEN. SEW ON THE RIBBONS USING A BLIND STITCH. FINALLY TAKE THE FINIALS OFF THE POLE AND SLIP IT THROUGH THE POCKET

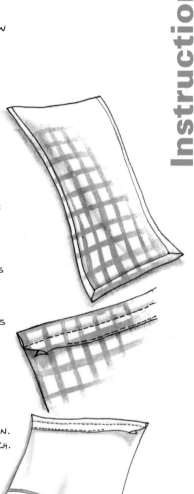

GINGHAM TEAMED UP WITH RIC-RAC ALWAYS MAKES
A GOOD COMBINATION ESPECIALLY IN A KITCHEN

Pocket Heading
Instructions

ESSENTIAL INGREDIENTS

POLE + BRACKETS

COTTON FABRIC

GINGHAM FOR POCKETS

RIC-RAC

PREPARATION

• CUT OUT YOUR CURTAINS WITH EXTRA AT THE TOP FOR A STAND — DOUBLED & ENOUGH FABRIC FOR THE POCKET FOR THE POLE TO GO THROUGH

• CUT 2 GINGHAM POCKETS

• YOU NEED 2 LARGER CIRCLES TO COVER THE FINIALS (ENDS) OF THE POLES

• CUT THE RIC – RAC – 4 WIDTHS & TURNINGS AND 2 LENGTHS & TURNINGS

MAKING A START

1. MAKE YOUR CURTAINS AS PAGE 13 (UNLINED) LEAVE TOP FOR THE MOMENT

2. MACHINE ON YOUR RIC-RAC

3. MACHINE A DOUBLE HEM AROUND GINGHAM POCKETS AND WITH A SECOND ROW CLOSE BY SEWING THE POCKETS IN PLACE — PRESS

4. TURN OVER THE TOP OF THE CURTAINS — YOU MUST REMEMBER TO ALLOW 2CM (1") STAND — BACK & FRONT & THEN MEASURE THE DIAMETER OF THE POLE AND ADD A LITTLE EXTRA FOR MOVEMENT. TURN RAW EDGE UNDER AT THE BACK & PIN, BASTE AND SEW 2 ROWS — THIS IS THE POCKET FOR THE POLE.

5. LASTLY, WITH YOUR CIRCLE OF CLOTH DO A BASTING STITCH AROUND IT AS IN THE DIAGRAM — POP IT OVER THE FINAL & PULL TIGHT — PERHAPS TIE A LITTLE RIC — RAC INTO A BOW TO SECURE?

Tab Headings

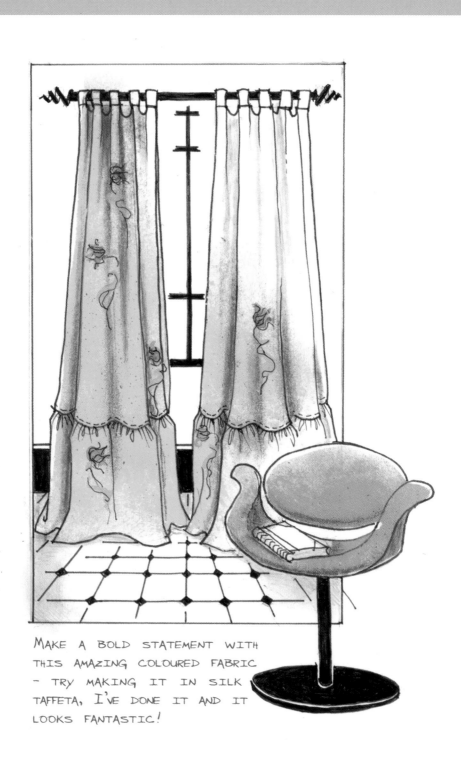

MAKE A BOLD STATEMENT WITH
THIS AMAZING COLOURED FABRIC
- TRY MAKING IT IN SILK
TAFFETA, I'VE DONE IT AND IT
LOOKS FANTASTIC!

ESSENTIAL INGREDIENTS
POLE & BRACKETS

FABRIC

WEIGHTS IF NEEDED

PREPARATION
- CUT YOUR TOP CURTAIN 2/3 OF OVERALL LENGTH AND THE BOTTOM 1/3
- CUT YOUR FRILLS DOUBLE THE WIDTH OF CURTAINS
- CUT THE TABS 5CM (2") WIDE x APPROXIMATELY 25CM (10") LONG
  – DEPENDING ON DIAMETER OF POLE

TIP: IT IS ADVISABLE ON A TAB HEADING TO LEAVE THE HEM UNFINISHED UNTIL YOU HAVE HUNG THE CURTAINS AS WITH THIS PARTICULAR HEADING THE LENGTH WILL VARY DEPENDING UPON THE LENGTH OF YOUR TABS.

MAKING A START

1. SEW YOUR TOP CURTAIN TOGETHER ALSO SEW YOUR FRILL PIECES TOGETHER, THEN USING A GATHERING STITCH, GATHER THE BOTTOM FRILL UNTIL IT IS SAME SIZE AS MAIN CURTAIN. SECURE THE STITCHING.

2. MAKE SURE THE GATHERING IS EVEN BEFORE PINING ON – BASTE AND MACHINE AS IN ILLUSTRATION. TURN OVER, PRESS AND TOP STITCH

3. SEW TABS UP AND TURN THROUGH, PRESS FLAT WITH THE SEAMS UNDERNEATH

4. PIN THE TABS IN PLACE EVERY 15CM (6")

5. TURN OVER THE TOP OF THE CURTAIN WITH THE TABS SECURED. MAKE A NARROW FACING 5CM (2") WIDE x THE WIDTH OF EACH CURTAIN TO HIDE ALL THE RAW EDGES AND SLIP STITCH ALL AROUND.

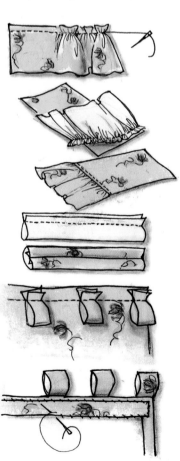

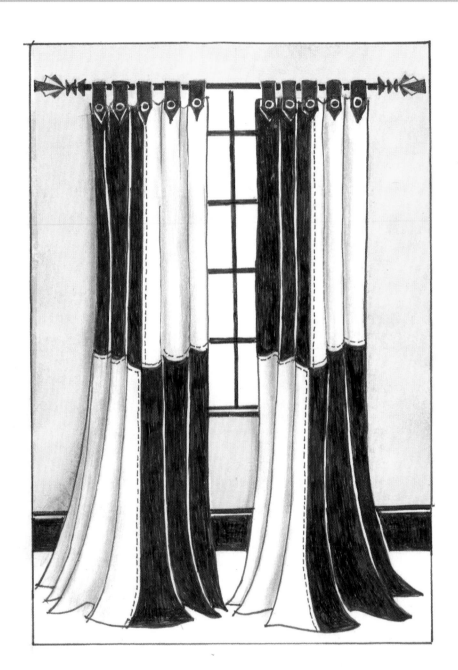

TRY OUT SOME DIFFERENT COLOUR COMBINATIONS — DO THE
SADDLE STITCHING BY HAND & THAT WAY YOU CAN SAY
YOU MADE AND DESIGNED THEM!

ESSENTIAL INGREDIENTS

FABRIC

CONTRAST FABRIC (EQUAL AMOUNTS)

LINING

EMBROIDERY SILK (TO SEW BY HAND)

PREPARATION

- THIS IS NOT AS HARD AS IT LOOKS!

- WHEN YOU WORK OUT YOUR MEASUREMENTS ADD AN EXTRA SEAM ALLOWANCE FOR THE WIDTH, AND ALSO FOR THE LENGTH. CUT ONE CURTAIN IN ONE COLOUR & THE OTHER IN THE CONTRAST - CUT THESE EACH INTO 4 & THEN SWAP THEM OVER TO MAKE THE CHEQUERED EFFECT - EASY!

- CUT YOUR TABS OUT ABOUT 8CM (3") × 35CM (14") LONG - DEPENDING ON THE DIAMETER OF THE POLE. CUT TWO FOR EACH TAB.

MAKING A START

1. BASTE BOTTOM PIECES TOGETHER, STITCH + PRESS OPEN FOLLOWED BY TOP PIECES & FINALLY JOIN TOPS + BOTTOMS TOGETHER. WHEN ALL SEAMS ARE PRESSED, WITH RIGHT SIDE FACING YOU, SADDLE STITCH NEAR TO THE SEAM WITH EMBROIDERY SILK IN CONTRAST. MAKE CURTAINS UP AS FOR LINED CURTAINS PAGE 14 LEAVING TOP OPEN.

2. TO MAKE TABS - LAY 2 PIECES RIGHT SIDES TOGETHER & SEAM AROUND 3 SIDES. THEN TURN & PRESS

3. TO ATTACH TO CURTAIN, PIN THE TABS TO TOP RIGHT SIDE IF THE CURTAIN & STITCH ACROSS

4. TURN TABS UP & SECURE TOP OF LINING WITH SLIP STITCH

5. TRY TABS ROUND POLE TO DECIDE HOW TO POSITION BUTTONS

Tie Heading – Voile

TRANSLUCENT CURTAINS ARE THE BEST THING SINCE SLICED BREAD. THEY CAN 'DRESS' AN UGLY WINDOW, DIFFUSE HARD LIGHT AND HIDE AN UNSIGHTLY VIEW.

ESSENTIAL INGREDIENTS
POLE AND BRACKETS

SHEER FABRIC

RIBBONS

WEIGHTS FOR HEM, IF NEEDED

TIPS: TRY TO BUY VERY WIDE VOILE THEN YOU WILL HAVE LESS
SEAMS USE A COLOURED COTTON FOR BASTING ON A VOILE FABRIC

PREPARATION

- SEW YOUR CURTAINS TOGETHER AS UNLINED FOUNDATIONS PAGE 13
  BUT LEAVE THE TOP UNDONE UNTIL LATER

- CUT YOUR RIBBONS 8 × WIDTH OF CURTAINS PLUS SEAM ALLOWANCES
  AND 2 × 15CM (6") FOR EACH TIE – YOU WILL NEED TIES
  APPROXIMATELY EVERY 16CM (6")

MAKING A START

1. FRENCH SEAM YOUR CURTAIN, IF
   POSSIBLE, OTHERWISE OVERLOCK
   AS USUAL

2. PLACE YOUR 1ST RIBBON ON THE
   HEM THEN MEASURE AND PIN ON
   THE NEXT 2 ROWS. BASTE AND
   MACHINE OR HAND STITCH WITH
   A BLIND STITCH (PAGE 11)

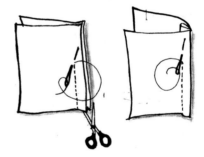

3. TURN OVER THE TOP OF THE
   CURTAIN, SLIP STITCH AND
   PRESS. NOW PIN YOUR TOP
   RIBBON IN PLACE POPPING
   YOUR 2 TIES IN EVERY 15CM
   (6") OR SO – BASTE & MACHINE.

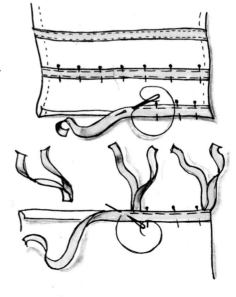

Tie Heading

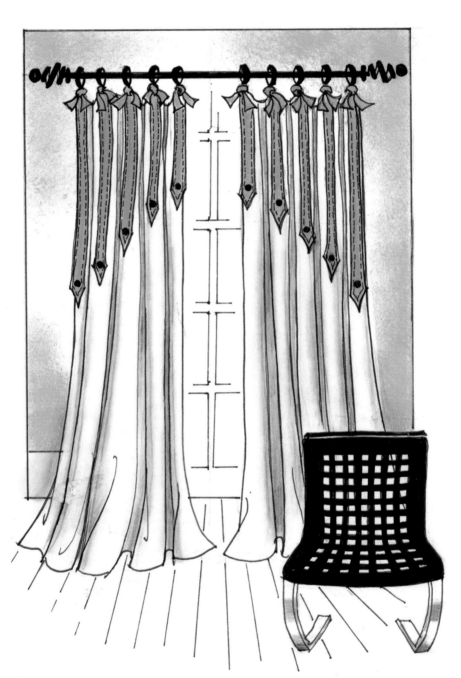

CONTRAST TABS COULD BE MADE WITH EMBROIDERED RIBBONS
— FOOD FOR THOUGHT!

ESSENTIAL INGREDIENTS

MAIN FABRIC – USE A FABRIC LIKE LINEN FOR THIS DESIGN

CONTRAST FABRIC

BUTTONS

PREPARATION

- TAKE THE MEASUREMENT OF YOUR CURTAINS AND DRAW ONTO GRAPH PAPER THIS WAY YOU CAN WORK OUT THE LENGTHS OF YOUR TABS WHICH WILL VARY ACCORDING TO THE WIDTH OF YOUR CURTAIN. TABS SHOULD BE ABOUT 5CM (2") WIDE AGAIN DEPENDING ON YOUR INDIVIDUAL CURTAIN – AND YOU WILL NEED 2 OF EACH – PER CURTAIN. ALSO CUT A SHORTER TIE x2 FOR EVERY TAB.

- MAKE CURTAINS AS UNLINED ONE ON PAGE 13

MAKING A START

1. LAY ALL THE PAIRS OF TABS TOGETHER RIGHT SIDES TOGETHER – PIN & BASTE THEN MACHINE ALL AROUND EXCEPT THE TOPS. CUT OFF ANY EXCESS FABRIC AND SNIP POINTS – SEE PAGE 12. PRESS FLAT.

2. PIN TABS INTO POSITION, PUSHING A SHORT TAB IN BEHIND EACH LONG ONE ABOUT 2CM (1"). BASTE AND TOP STITCH QUITE CLOSE TO THE EDGE AS IN DIAGRAM. FINALLY SEW ON THE BUTTONS.

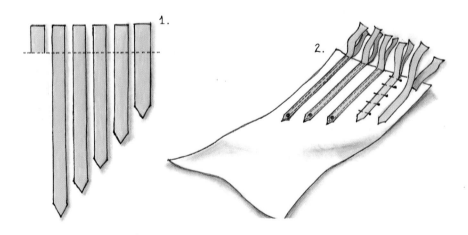

Tie-ons

TRY USING A PASTEL SILK FOR THIS
DELICATE DESIGN AND DECORATE IT
WITH HUGE BEADS AND CRYSTALS

ESSENTIAL INGREDIENTS
STEEL POLE & BRACKETS

MAIN CURTAIN FABRIC

CONTRAST FABRIC

BOBBLE EDGED TRIMMING

PREPARATION

- THE TOP 'SKIRT' NEEDS TO BE CUT ON THE CROSS (SEE PAGE 63 DIAGRAM A). IF THE FABRIC IS NARROW YOU WILL NEED TO HAVE A JOIN

- CUT OUT MAIN CURTAINS + YOUR TIES – ABOUT 2CM (1") WIDE AND 20CM (8") LONG. ALLOW 1 PAIR EVERY 15CM (6")

- CUT THE FACING FOR BOTH CURTAINS – A STRIP OF FABRIC THE WIDTH OF EACH ONE AND ABOUT 10CM (4") DEEP

MAKING A START

1. MAKE THE TOP SKIRT AND THE MAIN CURTAINS AS FOR UNLINED CURTAINS PAGE 13. LEAVE THE TOP EDGES UNFINISHED

2. MAKE THE TIES BY PRESSING THE FABRIC IN HALF AND THEN IN QUARTERS (SEE DIAGRAM). PRESS IN SHORT ENDS AND MACHINE ALL AROUND

3. LAY BOTH PIECES OF FABRIC DOWN RIGHT SIDES UP AND LAY THE TIES ACROSS THE TOP. PIN, BASTE AND LASTLY SEW THROUGH THE TIES

4. FOLD OVER THE RAW EDGE AT THE TOP AND PRESS – NOW PLACE YOUR FACING OVER THE RAW EDGE AND SLIP STITCH ALL AROUND TO NEATEN

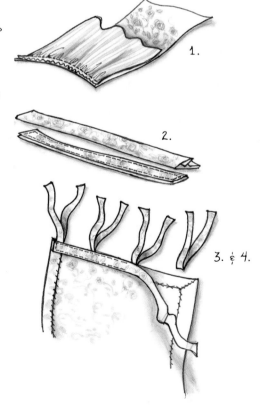

1.

2.

3. & 4.

Tie Headings

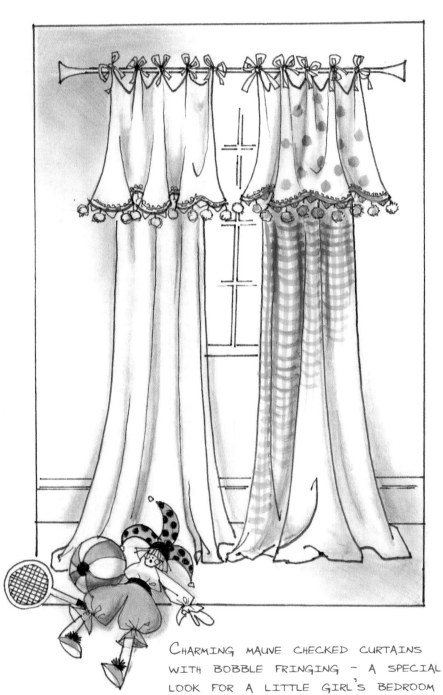

CHARMING MAUVE CHECKED CURTAINS
WITH BOBBLE FRINGING — A SPECIAL
LOOK FOR A LITTLE GIRL'S BEDROOM

ESSENTIAL INGREDIENTS
STEEL POLE & BRACKETS

MAIN CURTAIN FABRIC

CONTRAST FABRIC

BOBBLE EDGED TRIMMING

PREPARATION
- THE TOP 'SKIRT' NEEDS TO BE CUT ON THE CROSS (SEE DIAGRAM A)
  IF THE FABRIC IS NARROW YOU WILL NEED TO HAVE A JOIN

- CUT OUT MAIN CURTAINS + YOUR TIES — ABOUT 2CM (1") WIDE
  AND 20CM (8") LONG. ALLOW 1 PAIR EVERY 15CM (6")

- CUT THE FACING FOR BOTH CURTAINS — A STRIP OF FABRIC THE
  WIDTH OF EACH ONE AND ABOUT 10CM (4") DEEP

MAKING A START
1. MAKE THE TOP SKIRT AND THE MAIN
   CURTAINS AS FOR UNLINED CURTAINS
   PAGE 13. LEAVE THE TOP EDGES
   UNFINISHED

2. MAKE THE TIES BY PRESSING THE
   FABRIC IN HALF AND THEN IN
   QUARTERS (SEE DIAGRAM). PRESS IN
   SHORT ENDS AND MACHINE ALL AROUND

3. LAY BOTH PIECES OF FABRIC DOWN RIGHT
   SIDES UP AND LAY THE TIES ACROSS THE
   TOP. PIN, BASTE AND LASTLY SEW THROUGH
   THE TIES

4. FOLD OVER THE RAW EDGE AT THE TOP
   AND PRESS — NOW PLACE YOUR FACING
   OVER THE RAW EDGE AND SLIP STITCH
   ALL AROUND TO NEATEN

A.

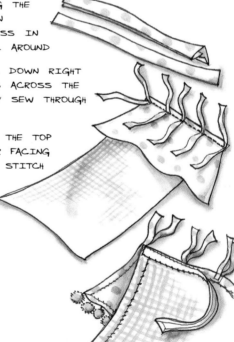

Eyelet Tops

A NAUTICAL FEEL

ESSENTIAL INGREDIENTS

POLE & BRACKETS

STRONG FABRIC LIKE SAIL CLOTH OR DENIM

EYELET HOLE MACHINE (2 SIZE HOLES)

ROPE OR CORD

PREPARATION
- CUT OUT THE TOP 2 CURTAINS WITH THE USUAL SEAM & HEM ALLOWANCES + AN EXTRA 13CM (5") FOR THE TOP SO THAT FABRIC IS DOUBLE FOR ADDED STRENGTH

MAKING A START!
1. MAKE UP 4 PARTS OF THE CURTAINS — MAKING A DOUBLE 2CM (1") HEM ALL AROUND EACH PART — YOU WILL NEED TO MITRE YOUR CORNERS — SEE PAGE 13

2. THEN TURN OVER THE TOP CURTAIN BY 13CM (5") AND STITCH ACROSS 2CM (1") DOWN

3. PUT THE TOP & BOTTOM CURTAIN TOGETHER FACE DOWN AND MARK YOUR EYELET HOLES AT THE TOP & MAKING SURE TOP & BOTTOM MATCH IN THE MIDDLE. START THE HOLES 5CM (2") IN FROM THE SIDES AND LEAVE A GAP OF ROUGHLY 10CM (4") BETWEEN EACH ONE.

4. LASTLY LACE UP YOUR CURTAIN!

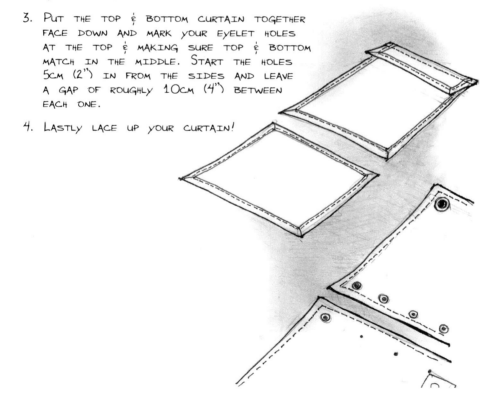

Eyelet Tops

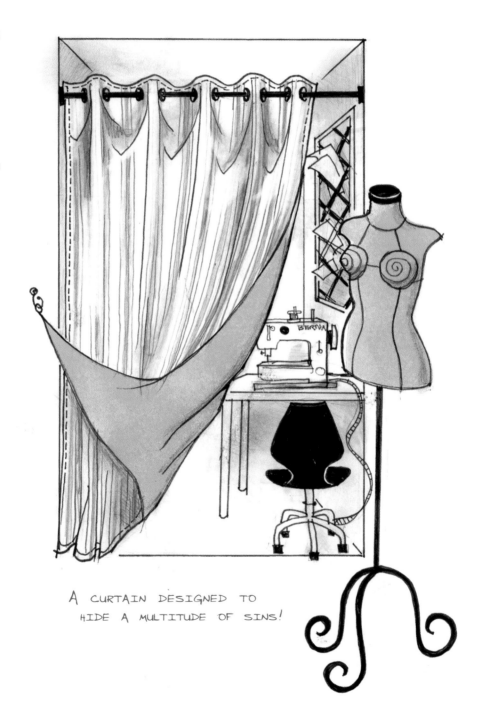

A CURTAIN DESIGNED TO
HIDE A MULTITUDE OF SINS!

ESSENTIAL INGREDIENTS
FABRIC

CONTRAST FABRIC

STRIP OF BUCKRAM

EYELET HOLE MACHINE

HOOK & RING & CURTAIN RAIL

PREPARATION

- FIX YOUR CURTAIN RAIL IN RECESS

- CHECK YOUR MEASUREMENTS BEFORE CUTTING FABRIC

- CUT BOTH FABRICS THE SAME SIZE PLUS SEAM ALLOWANCES

MAKING A START

1. PUT THE 2 FABRICS RIGHT SIDES TOGETHER, PIN & BASTE TOGETHER THE HEM & 2 SIDES. MACHINE, TURN THROUGH AND PRESS. TURN OVER THE TOP AND SLIP YOUR BUCKRAM JUST INSIDE THE 'SANDWICH' TOP AND THEN SLIP STITCH ALONG THE OPENING CATCHING THE BUCKRAM AT THE SAME TIME.

1.

2. MARK YOUR EYELET HOLE POSITIONS 5CM (2") DOWN FROM THE TOP & STARTING 5CM (2") IN FROM THE SIDE SEAMS THEN APPROXIMATELY 10CM (4") APART DEPENDING ON YOUR WIDTH OF CURTAIN. THREAD YOUR CURTAIN ON THE POLE & SECURE THE ENDS. LASTLY SEW A RING ON THE CORNER AT BOTTOM OF CURTAIN AND LOOP OVER YOUR HOOK TO HOLD IT BACK.

2.

Voile – Tension Wires

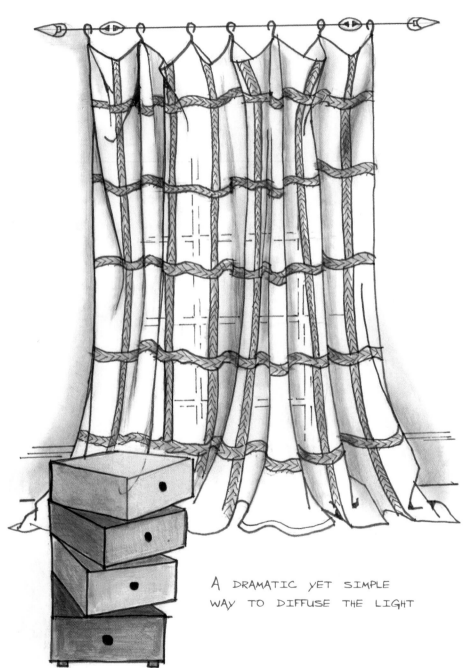

A DRAMATIC YET SIMPLE
WAY TO DIFFUSE THE LIGHT

ESSENTIAL INGREDIENTS

VOILE – BUY THE WIDEST YOU CAN FIND

GRAPH PAPER

SET SQUARE & METAL RULER

MARKER (NOT A PEN)

BRAID

CHAIN WEIGHTS

PREPARATION

● PUT UP YOUR WIRE SYSTEM

● ON YOUR GRAPH PAPER WORK YOUR PATTERN OUT

● CUT UP YOUR BRAID & ALLOWANCES

● CUT YOUR CURTAIN FABRIC

MAKING A START

1. MAKE UP YOUR BASIC CURTAIN AS PAGE 13
   – PUT IN THE WEIGHTS BEFORE THE SEWING
   HEM AS PAGE 79. LAY YOUR MADE UP CURTAIN
   FLAT ON THE TABLE AND WITH YOUR METAL
   RULER AND SET SQUARE MARK YOUR RIBBON
   POSITIONS. START SEWING YOUR BRAID
   ON FROM THE HEM WORKING TO
   YOUR PLAN ON THE GRAPH PAPER.
   PIN & BASTE ON THE
   HORIZONTAL BRAIDS. FIRST
   MACHINE THE HORIZONTAL BRAIDS
   AND THEN THE VERTICAL ONES,
   MAKING SURE THEY TURN OVER AT
   THE TOP AND AT THE HEM

2. SEW ON HOOKS AND HANG ON THE WIRE

TIP USE A LOOSE STITCH TO MACHINE THE
BRAID ONTO THE VOILE AS OTHERWISE IT WILL
PUCKER BADLY – IF YOU ARE A LADY OF LEISURE
YOU COULD SEW THE BRAID ON BY HAND!

Contemporary Curtains
Voile – Tension Wire

Voile – Tension Wire

IF YOU HAVE A VIEW LIKE THIS FROM YOUR APARTMENT WHO NEEDS CURTAINS!

ESSENTIAL INGREDIENTS

TENSION WIRE TRACKING & HOOKS (CHECK INSTRUCTIONS)

VOILE OR PARACHUTE SILK – (AS WIDE AS POSSIBLE)

HEAVY WEIGHTS TO HOLD FABRIC WHEN CUTTING OUT

GRAPH PAPER, METAL RULER, TAILOR'S CHALK OR PENCIL

PREPARATION

- CUT YOUR FABRIC TO SAME SIZE AS THE WINDOW, ADD EXTRA FOR SEAM ALLOWANCES PLUS A BIT FOR LUCK – SEAM UP THE MAIN CURTAIN

- DRAW YOUR CURTAIN SHOWING ALL SEAMS ON YOUR GRAPH PAPER. THEN INK IN YOUR OWN DESIGN – MAKE SURE YOUR RIBBONS WILL COVER THE SEAMS. ONCE YOU HAVE DRAWN THE DESIGN IT'S UP TO YOU TO TEST YOUR MATHS – YOU CAN ALSO DO THIS ON YOUR COMPUTER OF COURSE.

MAKING A START

1. SIMPLY MACHINE ON YOUR RIBBONS FOLLOWING THE DESIGN AND OVERLAPPING THEM – THEN TURN IN AND PRESS A SMALL HEM ALL AROUND CURTAIN & SLIP STITCH EDGES

2. HOOK YOUR RINGS ON TO THE TENSION WIRE

TIP SEW THE VERTICAL RIBBONS ON FIRST AND THEN THE HORIZONTAL ONES AS YOU CAN COVER THE RAW EDGES OF THE RIBBON.

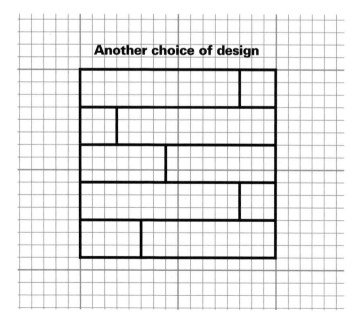

Another choice of design

Clip-on Heading

CLIP ON VALANCE IS A MODERN
APPROACH TO A TRADITIONAL STYLE

ESSENTIAL INGREDIENTS

FABRIC

CONTRAST FABRIC

CURTAIN TRACK (FACE FIX)

POLE AND BRACKETS

PENCIL PLEATED HEADING TAPE

RINGS WITH CLIPS

PREPARATION

- PUT THE TRACKING INTO POSITION – ALSO THE POLE, YOU MAY NEED TO BRING POLE AWAY FROM WALL SO THAT YOUR CURTAINS PULL PROPERLY BEHIND. (TWO WOODEN BLOCKS BEHIND THE BRACKETS WILL WORK).

- WORK YOUR MEASUREMENTS OUT FOR THE MAIN CURTAINS INCLUDING SEAM ALLOWANCES – CUT, PIN BASTE AND MAKE AS PAGE 13 – PUT ON HEADING TAPE AS PAGE 35 AND HANG IN PLACE.

- CUT A TEMPLATE FOR THE VALANCE THE ACTUAL SIZE OF THE POLE. TAKE THE MEASUREMENTS AS INDICATED ON PAGE 124 AND CUT YOUR SHAPE. CLIP THE TEMPLATE ONTO THE POLE TO SEE IF IT LOOKS IN PROPORTION – ADJUST ACCORDINGLY. MAKE A SECOND ELONGATED TEMPLATE BY JUST MULTIPLYING THE 1ST WIDTH BY 1.5, THEN TRANSFER THE MEASUREMENTS FROM THE 1ST TEMPLATE. (SEE PAGE 124). CUT OUT THE VALANCE.

- CUT OUT YOUR 3 BANDS FOR THE HEM THE SAME SHAPE AS THE ELONGATED VALANCE – ALLOWING 2 SEAMS ALLOWANCES BETWEEN THE 3 PIECES.

MAKING A START

1. JOIN YOUR VALANCE PIECES TOGETHER

2. JOIN YOUR 3 PIECES OF BORDER AS IN DIAGRAM 2 – MAKE SURE YOU PUT A STRAIGHT BORDER PIECE EITHER END OF THE CRESCENT SHAPE – BE SURE YOU HAVE CUT A 45 DEGREE ANGLE – CUT AWAY ANY SURPLUS FABRIC.

3. PRESS FLAT, THEN TURN IN AND PRESS A 1.5CM HEM TO THE WRONG SIDE – ALL ALONG BOTH BORDERS. SNIP CRESCENT BORDER (SEE DIAGRAM 3)

4. ON THE MAIN PART OF THE VALANCE, WRONG SIDE UP, PRESS OVER A 1.5CM HEM AND SNIP THE CURVES.

5. PIN THE BORDER ONTO THE MAIN VALANCE, BASTE AND STITCH INTO POSITION (SEE DIAGRAM 5)

6. FINISH THE VALANCE BY TURNING OVER THE HEM AT TOP AND HEMMING THE SIDES – THEN SIMPLY CLIP IT ON TO THE POLE.

1.

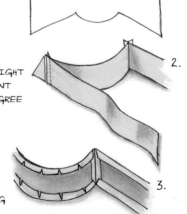
2.

3.

4.

5.

FABRIC PANELS LIKE THIS CAN BE USED FOR
MANY PURPOSES — TO DIFFUSE THE LIGHT, AS
ROOM DIVIDERS OR AS IN THIS CASE, LIKE A
HANGING PICTURE TO ADD COLOUR TO A ROOM

Room Dividers
Instructions

ESSENTIAL INGREDIENTS
MAIN FABRIC

CONTRAST FABRIC (DOUBLE AMOUNTS AS ALSO FOR FACINGS)

EMBROIDERY SILK FOR STITCHING

BAMBOO POLES – CHAINS AND CEILING HOOKS

TIP: MAKE YOUR CONTRAST TOP LONGER THAN NEEDED SO YOU CAN ADJUST LATER

PREPARATION
- MAKE A PAPER TEMPLATE AS TOP DIAGRAM – I SUGGEST ABOUT $\frac{1}{8}$TH OF THE TOTAL LENGTH OF THE PANEL × THE WIDTH

- CUT 2 CONTRAST PIECES FROM THE TEMPLATE.

- CUT 2 WIDE BANDS FOR THE HEM, THE WIDTH X ABOUT 15CM (6") BUT THIS WILL DEPEND ON YOUR WIDTH OF PANEL.

MAKING A START.
1. MAKE YOUR PANELS AS PAGE 13 BUT LEAVE THE TOPS UNFINISHED.

Template

2. ATTACH THE 1ST CONTRAST PIECE TO THE MAIN FABRIC, FACE TO FACE, PRESS THE SEAM OPEN – PLACE 2ND PIECE FACE TO FACE WITH THIS AND PIN, BASTE AND MACHINE AROUND THE CURVES. SNIP SEAMS (SEE DIAGRAM) TURN THROUGH AND PRESS FLAT. TURN YOUR TABS OVER TO THE BACK OF THE PANEL TO MAKE A LOOP TUCKING UNDER THE BACK FACING. (CHECK LENGTH IS O.K. BEFORE YOU SEW). FINALLY SEW INTO PLACE

3. TAKE THE WIDE BANDS FOR THE BOTTOM AND PRESS UNDER THE RAW EDGES AND PIN INTO POSITION. MACHINE ON.

4. SADDLE STITCH THE CONTRAST FABRIC AREAS WITH YOUR CONTRAST EMBROIDERY SILK ABOUT 1CM ($\frac{1}{2}$") FROM THE EDGE.

Lace Panel Room Divider

A FABULOUS LACE PANEL WHICH
SIMPLY RELIES ON ITS VIBRANT
COLOUR AND EXQUISITE VICTORIAN
LACE PATTERN

ESSENTIAL INGREDIENTS
CURTAIN AND POLE BRACKETS

LACE PANEL — THESE ARE OFTEN TO BE FOUND IN ANTIQUE MARKETS — BUT GET TO THE MARKET EARLY AS THEY ARE POPULAR AND SOON GET SNAPPED UP. MAKE SURE YOU HAVE THE WINDOW MEASUREMENTS TO HAND AS YOU MAY NOT HAVE TIME TO HESITATE

PREPARATION
- FIX POLE & BRACKETS

- MEASURE LENGTH & WIDTH FOR LACE PANEL

LOTS OF TIPS
TRY TO FIND A PANEL THE EXACT SIZE OF YOUR WINDOW FRAME THEN YOU WILL NOT LOOSE ANY OF THE DELICATE PATTERN BY HAVING TO HEM IT. DON'T WORRY IF IT'S TOO LONG — THEY LOOK GREAT 'PUDDLING' ON THE FLOOR!

VIBRANT COLOURS — THE ANTIQUE LACE YOU BUY WILL ALMOST CERTAINLY BE OFF WHITE. BUY A COLD WATER DYE AND FOLLOW THE INSTRUCTIONS.

I ALWAYS DYE MY LACE CURTAINS IN THE BATH SO THE DELICATE FABRIC CAN FLOAT AROUND AND WON'T BE DAMAGED BY A MACHINE. LET IT DRY IF POSSIBLE IN THE OPEN AIR — IT'S HOW IT'S DONE IN INDIA!

WHEN YOU WASH YOUR LACE PANEL, AGAIN DO IT IN THE BATH AND HANG UP WHEN STILL DAMP — IF THERE IS ANY SHRINKAGE — PULL FABRIC BACK TO CORRECT SIZE

MAKING A START
1. THERE IS A MINIMAL AMOUNT OF SEWING HERE — JUST TURNOVER THE TOP OF THE LACE ALLOWING 2CM (1") FOR STAND DOUBLED AND THEN ALLOW FOR THE THICKNESS OF THE DIAMETER OF THE POLE. SEW 2 ROWS OF STITCHING TO FORM THE POCKET AND SLIDE THE POLE THROUGH

Voile / Sheer

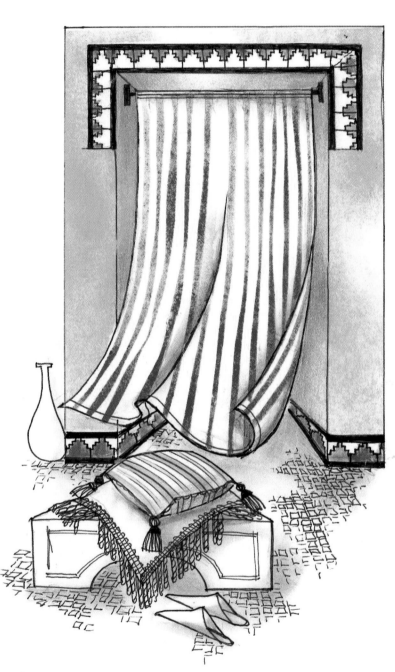

A SIMPLE PANEL IN A SHEER FABRIC, OFTEN USED
IN THE MEDITERRANEAN IN PLACE OF A DOOR

Voiles / Sheers
Instructions

ESSENTIAL INGREDIENTS
FABRIC – VOILE

CURTAIN RAIL WITH FIXING FOR A RECESSED DOOR

CHAIN WEIGHTS

PREPARATION
WHEN WORKING OUT YOUR FABRIC NEED DON'T FORGET TO ALLOW FOR A STAND 2CM (1") DOUBLED & ABOUT 4CM (1½") FOR POLE SIZE

AS THIS PANEL IS UNLINED IT WOULD BE EASY TO OVERLOCK ALL SEAMS AFTER CUTTING OUT

TIP TO MAKE THE PANEL FALL STRAIGHT ADD SOME WEIGHTS TO THE HEM. THE BEST TYPE FOR A VOILE CURTAIN IS MOST DEFINITELY A CHAIN. THE METAL CHAIN WILL SHOW THROUGH SO YOU MUST MAKE A SMALL SAUSAGE OF FABRIC TO HIDE THE CHAIN AS IN DIAGRAM.

MAKING A START
1. AS YOUR PANEL IS OVERLOCKED ON ALL SEAMS ALL YOU NOW HAVE TO DO IS TO LAY YOUR CHAIN ON THE HEM AS TOP DIAGRAM

1.

2. NOW STITCHING HEM AND SIDES IN THE USUAL WAY BY HAND OR MACHINE AND PRESS FLAT

3. FINALLY TURN OVER TOP OF CURTAIN AND MAKE A POCKET FOR YOUR CURTAIN ROD – SEE PAGE 49

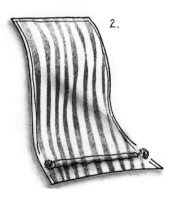

2.

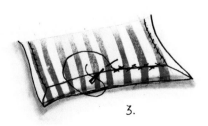

3.

Fabric Panels
Sliding Panels

Sliding Panels

PERHAPS EACH PANEL COULD
BE IN A DIFFERENT COLOUR?

Essential ingredients
Sliding panel tracking (ceiling fix)

Fabric

Wide ribbon

Weights for hem

Preparation

- I suggest you get a professional to put up this tracking, it's ceiling fixed and needs to be very secure — if not read the instructions very carefully!

- Cut out your 3 panels — usual seam allowances top, hem & sides. (These panels look best a fraction off the floor so that they fall straight)

Tip: Use a strong fabric like linen, if not these panels must be lined

Making a start

1. Mark the positions of the ribbons — be sure you get them straight — use a metal ruler and set square for accuracy. Pin the ribbons into place and then baste, machine & press. Use this panel to mark ribbon position for the other 2 panels.

2. Make up the 3 panels as in the unlined curtains, page 13 — or as page 14 if lined.

3. Before you close the mitres in the bottom corners pop your weights in — it does help to make the panels hang straight.

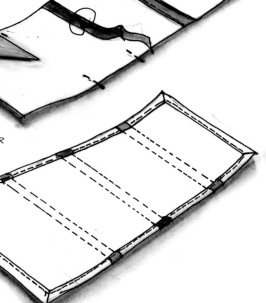

Using Trimmings

SIMPLE PANELS LIKE THIS CAN BE ADAPTED TO
OVERCOME VARIOUS OBJECTS LIKE RADIATORS

ESSENTIAL INGREDIENTS

POLE & BRACKETS

FABRIC & CONTRAST

WIDE BRAID

WEIGHTS (IN A STRIP)

PREPARATION

• PUT YOUR POLE & BRACKETS IN PLACE, CHECK YOUR MEASUREMENTS AGAIN

• DRAW YOUR 2 PANELS OUT ON GRAPH PAPER SO YOU CAN DECIDE WHERE TO PUT THE WIDE BRAID AND IT WILL HELP YOU WORK OUT FABRIC NEEDS

• CUT OUT YOUR 4 PANELS IN 2 DIFFERENT COLOURS ALSO CUT THE FACING FOR THE BACKS – THE SIZE OF THIS WILL DEPEND ON THE DIAMETER OF THE POLE

MAKING A START

1. STITCH THE TOP & BOTTOM TOGETHER ONE IN ONE COLOUR & THE OTHER IN THE CONTRAST. APPLY THE WIDE BRAID OVER THE SEAM LINES

2. SLIPSTITCH DOUBLE SIDE SEAMS LEAVING THE TOP OPEN, IN THE BOTTOM FOLD IN YOUR MITRES & CUT AWAY ANY EXCESS FABRIC – LAY THE CHAIN WEIGHT IN THE HEM FOLD THEN SLIPSTITCH IN PLACE

3. PLACE THE RIGHT SIDE OF THE FACING TO THE RIGHT SIDE OF PANEL – CUT A SMALL V IN THE CENTRE OF PANEL & FACING, PIN & BASTE THE FACING ON TO THE PANEL. MACHINE ALONG THE TOP & DOWN THE V. THEN TURN THE FACING OVER TO THE BACK AND PRESS

4. JUST BELOW THE V PUT YOUR 1ST ROW OF STITCHING FOR THE POCKET HEADING & THEN FOLD RAW EDGE UNDER AND PUT THE 2ND ROW OF STITCHING DEPENDING ON DIAMETER OF POLE

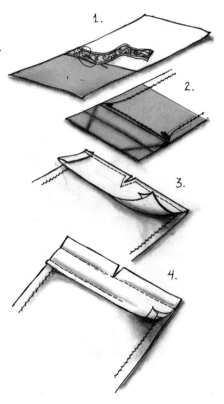

1.

2.

3.

4.

Clip On Heading

CHOOSE BIG CHECK RUGS — TRY TO
FIND MOHAIR CHUNKY ONES AS THEY ARE
NOT TOO HEAVY. OF COURSE IF YOU'RE
REALLY RICH YOU COULD USE A DESIGNER
CASHMERE CAR RUG AND FLAUNT IT!

Clip On Heading
Instructions

ESSENTIAL INGREDIENTS
POLE AND BRACKETS

HEAVY CLIPS AND RINGS TO MATCH POLE

2 BLANKETS OR RUGS WITH FRINGING BOTH ENDS

PREPARATION
- FIX POLE & BRACKETS

- MEASURE LENGTH FROM CLIPS TO THE FLOOR

TIPS BUY STRONG CLIPS AND USE MORE THAN USUAL AS RUGS CAN BE HEAVY – PUTTING CLIPS ON EVERY 10cm (4") EVEN THEN YOU MAY NEED MORE

MAKING A START
1. TURN OVER TOP OF RUG SO THAT IT IS CORRECT LENGTH AND THEN SIMPLY CLIP ON RINGS AND CLIPS AND PUT ON YOUR POLE...

...PIECE OF CAKE

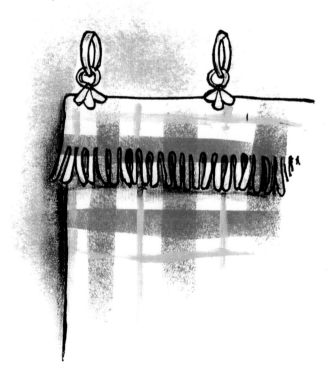

No Sew Café Curtains

CAFÉ CURTAINS WITH
NEATLY CLIPPED HEADINGS
ARE A QUICK AND SIMPLE
SOLUTION FOR KITCHEN AND
BATHROOM WINDOWS.

Essential ingredients
Piece of white tape

2 white cotton or linen handtowels

Thin curtain rods and holders

Sufficient rings and matching clips – allow 1 set every 10cm (4")
this will, of course, vary depending on width of each window

Preparation
• Make sure the poles, rings and clips are treated so they do not rust, as they will if you are using them in a damp area, such as a bathroom or kitchen. You can treat them yourself by coating them with a clear yacht varnish

Idea: It's great fun to use old-fashioned tea towels in place of white linen or small towelling hand towels in the bathroom

Making a start
1. Fix rod and brackets into 2 recessed windows

2. Slip the rings and clips on to each rod

3. Measure rod length and cut your piece of tape this length – one for each window

4. Turn over the top of each curtain to required length

5. Attach your tape to either side of curtain as this is the same width as your window you can put pleats to fit the tape size. Pop a pin into each pleat to hold it in place

6. Finally clip the clips on to the pinned pleats – now remove the pins and the tape....

   ....Finished!

Tie-on Curtains

DELICATE MUSLIN CURTAIN TIED ON WITH SATIN RIBBONS

Tie-on Curtains
Instructions

ESSENTIAL INGREDIENTS
THIN BRASS RAIL + SIDE FIXINGS (RECESS)

MUSLIN OR VOILE

RIBBONS IN VARIOUS COLOURS

PREPARATION
- FIX RAIL IN RECESS

- MEASURE THE WINDOW – YOU ONLY NEED TO ADD ON AN ALLOWANCE FOR A TURN OVER HEM AT THE TOP.

- MEASURE THE WIDTH OF THE WINDOW AND ALLOW 15CM (6") FOR EACH BUNCH AND THE SAME AGAIN FOR EACH GAP.

MAKING A START
1. TURN OVER TOP EDGES OF FABRIC ABOUT 5CM (2") AND PRESS

2. FRAY THE BOTTOM HEM BY PULLING OUT THREADS FROM THE FABRIC

3. CUT YOUR RIBBONS – ALLOW 25CM (10") EACH ONE X HOWEVER MANY BUNCHES.

4. BUNCH YOUR FABRIC STARTING AT THE TOP LEFT SIDE – PINCH 2 OR 3 PLEATS TOGETHER THEN TIE A RIBBON AROUND THE BUNCH – YOU MIGHT NEED THREE HANDS FOR THIS PART!

5. TIE RIBBONS ON TO THE RAIL....DONE!

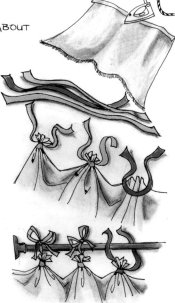

WHY COVER UP A STUNNING WINDOW LIKE THIS? PERHAPS
DIFFUSE THE LIGHT A LITTLE WITH A CRISP COTTON
'BLIND' SIMPLY MADE FROM A VICTORIAN TABLECLOTH AND
ADD A CRYSTAL HERE AND THERE FOR FUN.

Lace Blinds
Instructions

ESSENTIAL INGREDIENTS
TABLE CLOTH OR SIMILAR

CRYSTALS OR BEADS

STAPLE GUN — THE KIND YOU BUY IN ARTS + CRAFTS SHOP

NARROW VELVET OR SATIN RIBBON

ADHESIVE SUITABLE FOR FABRIC

SEWING KIT

TIPS LOOK IN MARKETS FOR CRISP WHITE VICTORIAN TABLECLOTHS OR PILLOWCASES WITH LACE EDGING. IF YOU CAN'T FIND ANYTHING WITH LACE ON, BUY IT SEPARATELY AND SEW IT ON

PREPARATION
- MEASURE THE WINDOW — THE FABRIC CAN ONLY BE ATTACHED TO A FLAT WOODEN SURFACE — THIS DESIGN WOULD BE NO GOOD IF THE WINDOW OPENS INWARDS

- ALLOW 3CM (1") EXTRA FOR TURNING IN ON TOP OF WINDOW AND FOR TWO SIDES

MAKING A START
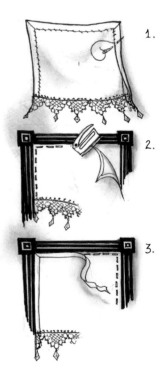

1. MITRE CORNERS OF CLOTH AS SHOWN IN SEWING TECHNIQUES. TURN IN SEAM ALLOWANCE AND PRESS FIRMLY WITH A FAIRLY HOT IRON. HEM STITCH 3 EDGES. SEW BEADS ON EDGE OF LACE

2. STAPLE FABRIC TO WOOD ON 3 EDGES

TIP BEFORE STAPLING FABRIC TO WOOD PRESS A LITTLE BLUE TACK HERE AND THERE TO HOLD THE FABRIC. IT CAN BE REMOVED AS YOU REACH IT WITH STAPLE GUN

3. GLUING — SQUEEZE A FINE LINE OF GLUE ON FABRIC ABOVE AND BELOW STAPLES. PRESS ON RIBBON AND HOLD DOWN FOR A MOMENT UNTIL GLUE 'TAKES' DON'T USE TOO MUCH GLUE!

Personal Touches

A.

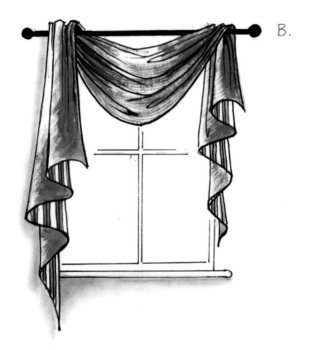

B.

Try adding a few personal touches to your windows

A. I HAVE A LOVELY ROUND WINDOW LIKE THIS IN MY HOUSE IN FRANCE AND I CHANGE THE THEME OF IT ALL THE YEAR ROUND. SPRING, I HAVE MIMOSA, IN THE SUMMER OLIVE BRANCHES AND AT CHRISTMAS LOTS OF IVY AND BERRIES.

B. YOU ONLY NEED TO CUT 2 PIECES OF FABRIC LIKE THIS AND SEW TOGETHER THEN TURN THROUGH AND PRESS. JUST SLIP STITCH THE OPEN ENDS AND DRAPE IT OVER YOUR POLE HOWEVER YOU WANT.

Using Trimmings

A WONDERFUL OVER THE TOP
WAY TO DRESS A WINDOW

ESSENTIAL INGREDIENTS
POLE AND BRACKETS

BATTEN & METAL BRACKETS

RINGS - CORD - CLEAT

TOUCH & CLOSE TAPE

WOODEN SLATS

WIDE BRAID - FRINGED BEADS

ROPE AND TASSELS

PREPARATION
- FIX POLE & BATTEN IN PLACE
- CUT FABRIC AND CONTRAST THE SAME SIZE

MAKING A START

1. LAY FABRIC AND CONTRAST FABRIC TOGETHER WITH RIGHT SIDES TOGETHER, SEAM ALL AROUND 3 SIDES, LEAVE THE TOP OPEN, TURN THROUGH AND PRESS

2. TURN OVER THE TOP OF THE CURTAIN WITH A NARROW HEM, PRESS AND THEN TURN OVER AGAIN TO MAKE A POCKET FOR THE POLE - THE SIZE OF POCKET DEPENDS ON POLE DIAMETER

3. MAKE ROMAN BLINDS AS ON PAGE 105

4. ATTACH THE BRAID & BEADS TO THE BLIND

5. FINALLY 'DRESS' THE CURTAIN - THE ROPE CAN KNOT OVER THE FINIAL - THEN FINISH OFF WITH LOADS OF DRIPPING BEADS!

Japanese Panel

KEEP THE VIEW — DIFFUSE THE LIGHT WITH
THIS SPECTACULAR APPLE BLOSSOM PANEL

ESSENTIAL INGREDIENTS

POLE & BRACKETS

FABRIC — TRANSLUCENT

CHAIN WEIGHTS FOR HEM

PREPARATION

- CUT OUT YOUR PANEL WITH USUAL HEM AND SIDE SEAM ALLOWANCES

- ALLOW EXTRA 2CM (1") FOR STAND

- CUT A FACING IN THE SAME FABRIC WITH A SEAM ALLOWANCE AT THE TOP & 2CM (1") STAND AND ENOUGH TO MAKE A POCKET FOR THE POLE DEPENDING ON ITS DIAMETER

MAKING A START

1. MAKE YOUR PANEL UP AS FOR UNLINED CURTAINS — JUST BEFORE SLIP STITCHING THE HEM PLACE YOUR CHAIN WEIGHTS ON THE FOLD LINE THEN MITRE AND STITCH CLOSED

2. PLACE YOUR FACING RIGHT SIDE TO RIGHT SIDE OF THE PANEL & CUT A SMALL V IN THE MIDDLE AT THE TOP, ABOUT 2CM (1"). PIN, BASTE & MACHINE, TURN THROUGH — PRESS FLAT

3. MACHINE JUST BELOW THE V ACROSS THE CURTAIN TO FORM THE TOP OF YOUR POCKET HEADING — ALLOW FOR SIZE OF POLE PLUS A LITTLE EXTRA FOR MOVEMENT — TURN RAW EDGE UNDER AND CATCH WITH YOUR SECOND ROW OF STITCHING — SLIP YOUR PANEL ON TO THE POLE

1.

2.

3.

With Loops + Hooks

PERHAPS YOU COULD CUT OUT THE LEOPARD?

ESSENTIAL INGREDIENTS
PLANK OF WOOD + NAILS

HOOKS & PEG

SHARP KNIFE (SCALPEL)

HEAVY BLANKET-TYPE FABRIC

CONTRAST LEOPARD PRINT

EMBROIDERY SILK

PREPARATION
- ALLOW 1½ WIDTHS OF BOTH FABRICS, IN THIS CASE, PLUS USUAL SEAM ALLOWANCES

MAKING A START

1. PUT THE 2 RIGHT SIDES OF THE FABRIC TOGETHER, PIN & BASTE THEN MACHINE BOTH SIDES AND HEM TOGETHER LEAVING THE TOP OPEN. TURN THROUGH FORMING A BAG AND PRESS.

2. CUT OUT A 10CM (4") FACING THE WIDTH OF THE CURTAIN IN YOUR MAIN FABRIC IN THIS CASE, THE CHECK AND MACHINE IT ON TO THE TOP WITH THE 2 RIGHT SIDES FACING. THEN WITH A SHARP KNIFE (OR SCALPEL) CUT SLITS IN THE FABRIC FOR THE ROPE TO COME THROUGH ABOUT 2CM (1") BIGGER THAN THICKNESS OF THE ROPE. EMBROIDER AROUND EACH SLIT WITH BLANKET STITCH (SEE PAGE 11)

3. TURNOVER YOUR FACING TO THE BACK OF THE CURTAIN AND PRESS A NARROW EDGE AS FOR A HEM AND SLIP STITCH IT DOWN LEAVING 2 ENDS OPEN. THREAD THE ROPE THROUGH THE POCKET MAKING SURE YOU HAVE A KNOT AT BOTH ENDS! NOW WITH A KNITTING NEEDLE OR SKEWER PICK OUT THE ROPE THROUGH THE BUTTON HOLES TO FORM YOUR LOOP. HANG UP & HOLD BACK WITH A PEG.

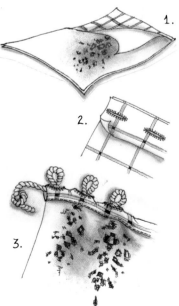

Fringed Shawl

THERE'S NOTHING TO IT — ALL YOU NEED IS STYLE

URTAIN
CIPES

Fringed Shawl
Instructions

101

Instructions

PREPARATION

- BANG 2 NAILS ONTO THE ARCHITRAVE OF YOUR WINDOW, THE BIGGER THE BETTER

- YOU MAY BE LUCKY ENOUGH TO FIND A WONDERFUL SHAWL IN AN ANTIQUE MARKET BUT JUST IN CASE NOT...

MAKING A START

1. CUT OUT YOUR SQUARE — BE GENEROUS, PERHAPS ADD ON ANOTHER — WIDTH AGAIN AND THE SAME ON THE LENGTH. TURN OVER DOUBLED NARROW HEM, PRESS AND SLIP STITCH ALL AROUND. PIN AND BASTE THE FRINGING ON THE RIGHT SIDE OF SQUARE AND THEN HAND SEW WITH BLIND STITCH ALL AROUND. DON'T BUY A CHEAP FRINGE — SPLASH OUT, IT'S WORTH IT

2. PIN ON SOME DRIED LAVENDER HELD TOGETHER WITH RAFFIA OR KNITTING WOOL

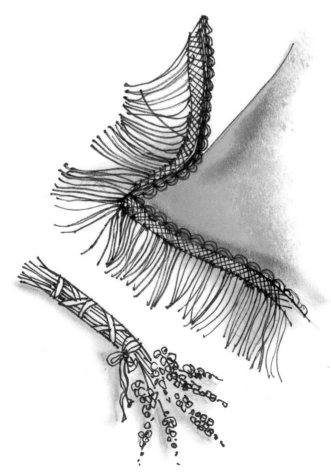

A Few Ideas

PERSONALLY I SUGGEST YOU GO TO YOUR
LOCAL STORE AND ORDER ONE TO BE MADE —
NOTHING LOOKS WORSE THAN A HOMEMADE BLIND
— JUST BUY A BASIC ONE AND EXPERIMENT

A Few Ideas
Instructions

A. DRAW YOUR DESIGN & SCRIBBLE ON THE BITS THAT WILL BE CUT OUT TO MAKE SURE IT WILL WORK AS A STENCIL. TRACE THE DESIGN ONTO THICK WAXED TRACING PAPER & CUT OUT WITH A SCALPEL. PUT DESIGN ONTO BLIND & SECURE WITH MASKING TAPE. APPLY PAINT WITH STENCIL BRUSH, ENSURING THAT YOU REMOVE EXCESS PAINT BY DABBING ON KITCHEN ROLL FIRST

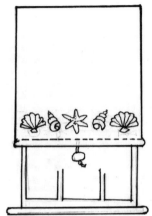

B. CUT OUT SQUARES OF FELT – MARK YOUR BLIND AND SIMPLE GLUE ON THE FELT PATCHES OR YOU CAN CUT A STENCIL AS ABOVE

C. WITH A RULER AND SET SQUARE MARK THE POSITIONS OF THE SQUARE HOLES ON THE BACK OF THE BLIND. CAREFULLY WITH A FIRM HAND CUT THE HOLES WITH A SCALPEL.

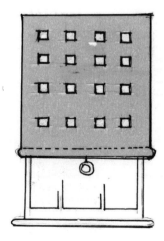

Variations

LET THE PRINT TAKE OVER — WHO CARES!

ESSENTIAL INGREDIENTS

FABRIC — LINING

BATTEN & BRACKETS

CORD — ALLOW 4 LENGTHS
& 2 WIDTHS OF BLIND

BRASS LOOPS 2 × EACH POCKET

2 VINEYES — CLEAT — CORD END

FLAT BATTEN (FOR HEM) & ROUNDED
DOWELS FOR POCKETS

TOUCH + CLOSE TAPE & STAPLE GUN

PREPARATION

- CUT YOUR FABRIC TO EXACT SIZE OF THE BLIND PLUS SEAM ALLOWANCES — AND THE SAME WITH THE LINING

- COVER THE BATTEN (SEE DIAGRAM BELOW)

- STAPLE ON 1 SIDE OF TOUCH & CLOSE TAPE TO FRONT EDGE

- PUT BATTEN IN PLACE WITH BRACKETS & SCREW IN 2 VINEYES

MAKING A START

1. WORK ON YOUR FACE (MAIN) FABRIC FIRST — PRESS SIDES & BOTTOM TURNINGS (SINGLE) — PUT TO ONE SIDE

2. PRESS IN THE SIDE TURNINGS — THE LINING WIDTH SHOULD BE ABOUT 5CM (2") NARROWER THAN YOUR FABRIC

3. MARK YOUR LINING, WITH TAILOR'S CHALK, WHERE YOU NEED TO PUT POCKETS. AS A ROUGH GUIDE MEASURE 10CM (4") UP FROM THE BOTTOM AND THAT IS WHERE 1ST ONE GOES THEN ABOUT 1 EVERY 25 – 30CM (10 – 12"). MAKE SURE THEY ARE EVENLY DISTRIBUTED.

4. MAKE YOUR POCKETS AS IN THE DIAGRAM & MACHINE ONTO THE LINING. POP YOUR ROUNDED DOWELS INTO EACH POCKET & THEN SLIP STITCH YOUR LINING TO THE MAIN FABRIC

5. TURN OVER THE RAW EDGE AT THE TOP OF THE BLIND AND SLIP STITCH O (HIDING THE RAW EDGE) THE SECOND SIDE OF THE TOUCH & CLOSE TAPE. PRESS 2 TAPES TOGETHER TO HANG THE BLIND.

6. LASTLY THREAD THE CORD THROUGH THE LOOPS AS IN DIAGRAM — THIS IS FOR A LEFT HAND PULL BLIND — PUT THE CORD END ON & FIX THE CLEAT TO THE WALL

Blinds For Small Windows

A.

B.

THEY BLOCK OUT SOME
LIGHT WHEN PUT INTO A
RECESSED WINDOW. BUT
THEY DO LOOK GOOD!

A. ESSENTIAL INGREDIENTS
FABRIC FOR BLIND AND CONTRAST STRIPE.

YOU NEED TO LOOK ON PAGE 105 FOR INGREDIENTS.

PREPARATION

1. CUT OUT THE MAIN FABRIC ALLOWING
   SEAM ALLOWANCES ON ALL SIDES, THEN
   CUT CONTRAST BORDERS AND SEAM
   ALLOWANCES ALSO ON ALL SIDES.

2. PIN SHORT ANGLED EDGES OF CONTRAST
   TOGETHER, STITCH, PIN AND BASTE THE
   SIDES AND THE BOTTOM TO THE MAIN
   PART OF THE BLIND – LAYING THE
   CONTRAST EDGES ON TO THE MAIN
   PART OF THE BLIND, RIGHT SIDES
   TOGETHER. STITCH AND PRESS.

3. CONTINUE TO MAKE THE BLINDS AS ON PAGE 105.

TIP: MEASURE YOUR RECESSED WINDOW WIDTH AT TOP,
MIDDLE AND BOTTOM JUST IN CASE THEY VARY AND MAKE
THE BLIND TO THE SMALLEST MEASUREMENT.

A.

B. ESSENTIAL INGREDIENTS
AS PAGE 105 BUT DIVIDE YOUR FABRIC
NEEDS IN 2

PREPARATION

- GO TO PAGE 105 FOR ROMAN BLINDS
  AND ADAPT TO SUIT YOUR WINDOW.

- FOR CHEQUERED DESIGNS LOOK AT PAGE 55
  TO SEE HOW TO MAKE OBVIOUSLY ADAPTING
  TO YOUR SIZES ETC.

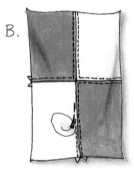

B.

Blinds With Valances

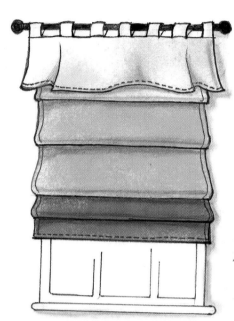

A.

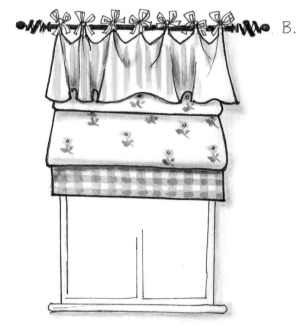

MAKE A PRETTY TOPPING FOR
YOUR BASIC ROMAN BLIND

B.

Instructions

ESSENTIAL INGREDIENTS

A.

POLE & BRACKETS

3 FABRICS ALL SAME QUANTITIES

LINING

ALSO SAME PARTS AS FOR ROMAN BLIND ON PAGE 105

PREPARATION

- WORK OUT YOUR FABRIC NEEDS AND DIVIDE THE LENGTH INTO 3 — ADD AN EXTRA SEAM ALLOWANCE FOR EACH CHANGE OF FABRIC

- CUT OUT YOUR VALANCE, ON THE CROSS. WORK OUT HOW MANY TABS YOU NEED SEE PAGE 55

MAKING A START

1. MAKE YOUR TABS AS DIAGRAM AND MACHINE ONTO VALANCE ON THE RIGHT SIDE & PRESS FLAT

2. TURN THE TABS OVER TO THE BACK, PRESS AGAIN AND THEN PUT THE LINING IN PLACE AND SLIPSTITCH ALL AROUND

3. HANG YOUR BLIND ONTO THE BATTEN AND SLIP YOUR VALANCE ONTO THE POLE

B.

1. MAKE BLIND AS PAGE 105 WITH EQUAL AMOUNTS OF 3 FABRICS AS ABOVE AND HANG

2. CUT YOUR VALANCE ON THE CROSS — DEPENDING ON THE FABRIC I WOULD CONSIDER NOT LINING THIS DESIGN AS IT LOOKS VERY SOFT WHEN CUT ON THE CROSS

3. MAKE YOUR RIBBONS FROM THE SAME MATERIAL AS THE VALANCE — TRY TO MAKE THEM AS NARROW AS POSSIBLE

A.

B.

Oriental Influence

ORIENTAL INFLUENCE

Instructions

ESSENTIAL INGREDIENTS
BATTEN

SCREWS

CLEAT

RINGS

TOUCH + CLOSE TAPE

FABRIC

PICOT RIBBON

GRAPH PAPER

PREPARATION
- CUT BLIND TO SIZE OF WINDOW ℮ SEAM ALLOWANCES

MAKING A START
1. USE GRAPH PAPER TO WORK OUT YOUR DESIGN FOR THE RIBBON SO THAT IT BALANCES WELL WITH THE SIZE OF YOUR WINDOW. (SCALE 1 SQUARE = 10CM)

2. TO POSITION RIBBON ACCORDING TO YOUR DESIGN, USE A SET SQUARE ℮ STEEL RULER + EITHER MARK ON FABRIC WITH TAILOR'S CHALK OR USE PINS. PIN, BASTE + FINALLY HAND SEW OR MACHINE STITCH RIBBON, ATTACHING VERTICAL PIECES FIRST SO THE ENDS ARE HIDDEN WHEN THE HORIZONTAL PIECES ARE APPLIED.

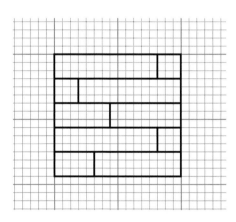

Relaxed Shades

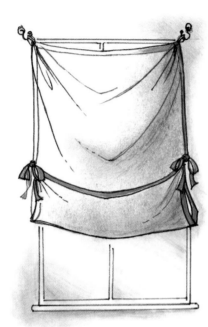

A. HESSIAN UNSTRUCTURED
   BLINDS WOULD FIT INTO
   MOST ROOMS WITHOUT
   BEING OBTRUSIVE

B. SACKING CAFÉ CURTAIN
   COST NEXT TO NOTHING
   BUT LOOKS GREAT

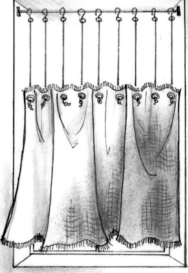

A. – Essential ingredients

2 hooks

Hessian fabric

Woven braid 5cm (2") wide

Preparation

- Cut the fabric to the size of your window to include the architrave. Add the usual seam allowances

- Cut braid long enough to go around the fabric plus perhaps 10cm (4") extra for mitreing etc. Cut 4 pieces of braid for ties & 2 for loops.

Making a start

1. Lay the hessian on the table and pin the braid on to the edge with the right side down, pin & baste. Mitreing the corners as you go. Machine and snip seams if necessary

2. Turn the braid over the raw edges and slip stitch all around

3. Sew 2 loops (braid) on to the top corners and sew 2 ties on to the bottom corners and the other half way up

B. – Essential ingredients

Curtain rod and fixings for recess

Sacking & wide webbing

String or rope

Hooks

Eyelet hole machine

Making a start

1. Cut your sacking to required size and pull out some threads at the top and the bottom to make fringing

2. Cut a length of webbing to the size of sacking to form a facing and sew onto the reverse – this is so the eyelet holes have something to punch into

3. Mark your eyelet holes – punch in the holes. Put string through the eyelet holes – knot and knot the other end onto the hook

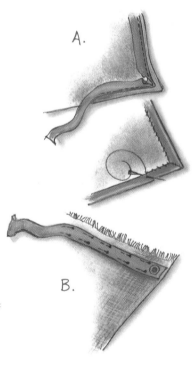

A.

B.

Tie Ons / Portiére Panels

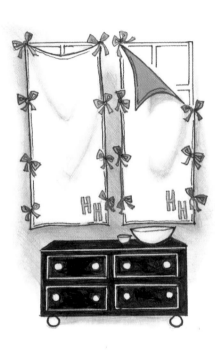

A. DELICIOUSLY SWEET
   BLINDS – JUST
   ADD YOUR OWN
   INITIALS

B. PORTIÉRE PANELS –
   MAKE THEM IN VOILE
   FOR PRIVACY

Instructions

A. Essential Ingredients
Hooks × 16

Main fabric

Equal amount of contrast fabric

16 ribbons each about 30cm (12") long

Preparation
- Fix your hooks into the architrave
- Cut out your 2 fabrics the size of the window plus seam allowances all around
- Mark the position of the ribbons (check the hook positions)

Making a start
1. Pin, baste the 2 fabrics face to face remembering to slip the doubled ribbons into the bag of the two fabrics as you go. When everything is in place, machine & turn through

2. Fold in your top and slip stitch

3. Machine near the edge all the way around the blind. Tie your ribbons onto the hooks

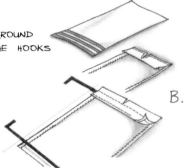

A.

B.

B. Essential ingredients
2 Portiére rods

Braids × 3 rows on each panel

Fabric- translucent

Preparation
- Cut your panels out, remember to allow extra length for the stand at the top plus a turn up on the hem the width of the portiére pole plus usual seam allowances
- Cut facing as page 97
- Cut 6 widths of ribbons & turn ins

Making a start
1. Sew the ribbons on the hem

2. turn up extra long hem, turn in raw edge and make a pocket heading for the portiére rod

3. then follow instructions on page 97

Roll Ups

JUST FOLLOW THE INSTRUCTIONS
ON THE REVERSE AND SIMPLY
'PINK' THE EDGES

ADD RIBBONS
IN YOUR OWN
TEAM COLOURS

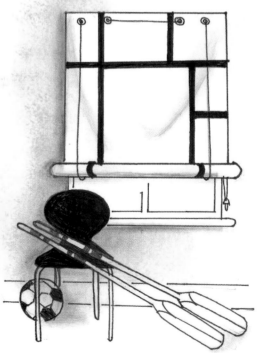

Essential ingredients
Firm fabric such as sail cloth or linen

Touch & close tape (width of blind)

Blind cord & cleat

Thin wooden dowel (width of blind)

Wooden batten

Screws with large eyelets

Eyelet kit

Long screws to hang batten

Preparation
• Cut the fabric the length of your window plus 25cm (10") for the hems & 5cm (2") for the sides

Making a start
1. Laying the fabric wrong side up press in 0.5cm (¼") turning down sides & then another 2cm (1") & press flat

• Make a double hem at the top of the blind 10cm (4") = turn over another 10cm (4"). Press, baste and machine

• Mark your two sets of eyelet holes – 1 set to be 5cm (2") down from top – start 15cm (6") from the side. Mark this then leave a 10cm (4") gap. Mark – then do exactly the same on the other side

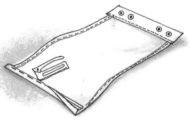

• Punch the 4 holes in with a fairly large size eyelet hole

• Staple the dowel rod to the bottom & raw edge of the blind – see diagram

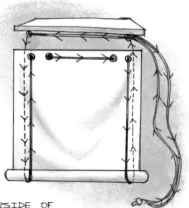

• Slip stitch the looped side of the touch – and – close tape to the back of the top of the blind. Cover the batten with fabric – see page 42 – then attach the batten to its correct position over the window with long screws – staple the other part of the touch & close tape to the batten.

2. Screw the 2 eyelet screws onto the underside of the batten in line with the eyelet holes on the blind. Attach the blind with the two sides of the touch & close tape. Now thread your cord starting from the cleat – just follow the arrows

Basic Cushions + a Few Ideas

1. MAKE 1 SIZE LARGER & TIE UP WITH STRING

2. WRAP UP LIKE A PARCEL

3. USE A NARROW BRAID

4. MACHINE ON THE RIBBONS BEFORE YOU MAKE THE CUSHION

5. SEW ON THE RIBBONS – MITRE THE CORNERS

6. CONTRAST BAND & SQUARE

7. CUT OUT SEGMENTS BUT DON'T FORGET SEAM ALLOWANCES

8. SEW ON THE BEADS & TIE THE BOW GOING THROUGH TO THE OTHER SIDE

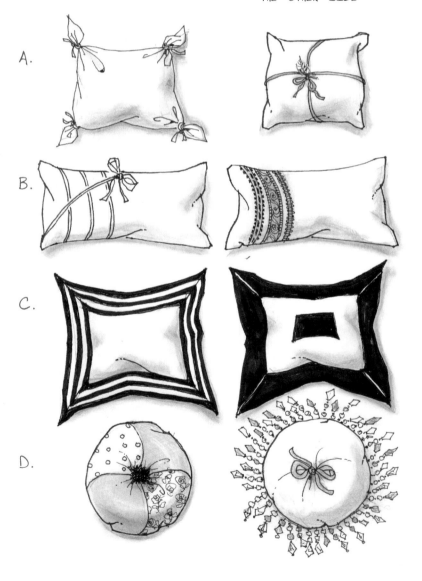

A.

B.

C.

D.

CURTAIN
RECIPES

Basic Cushions
Instructions

119

Instructions

A. Cut out 2 squares with seam allowances – put pieces face to face and machine 1 side leaving a gap for your zip. Press the seam flat, with the face cloth towards you put the zip under the opening and machine into place. Open the zip. Now machine the other 3 sides, turn through the opening & press flat

B. Cut your oblong cushion cover and follow instructions above

C. Cut 1 square an extra 20cm (8½") added and another square with 25cm (10") added & cut this in 2. Now make as A but put the zip into the centre seam (see diagram below) – machine an inner square the size of your cushion pad

D. Cut your circle out and machine fabric face to face – leave a gap for cushion pad to go through – press and put in pad then slip stitch gap up

SEWING IN THE ZIP

Table Covers

A. HEAVY BULLION FRINGING

ROWS OF VELVET RIBBON

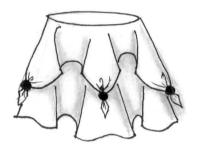

B. HUGE WOODEN BEADS

BEADED FRINGE

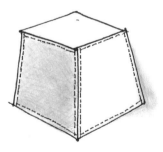

C. SADDLESTITCHED CUBE

CHEQUERS

INSTRUCTIONS

A.

- MEASURE YOUR TABLE FROM THE CENTRE TO THE FLOOR — DOUBLE IT AND ADD 2 SEAM ALLOWANCES. LAY YOUR FABRIC OUT FLAT AS IN DIAGRAM — YOUR FABRIC MAY BE WIDE ENOUGH BUT, IF NOT, FOLLOW THIS DIAGRAM

- ONCE YOU HAVE DRAWN YOUR CIRCLE, CUT THE EXTRA FABRIC AND SEAM ON TO THE MAIN BODY AS SHOWN

- PRESS A DOUBLE HEM ALL AROUND AND MACHINE EDGES

B.

- MAKE THE UNDER COVER AS A ABOVE

- FOR THE TOP CLOTH CUT YOUR FABRIC INTO A SQUARE

- TURN OVER A DOUBLE NARROW HEM AND PRESS FLAT

- MITRE THE CORNERS AS PAGE 13 — BASTE — LASTLY MACHINE ALL AROUND & PRESS

- BUY BIG BEADS — WITH BIG HOLES THEN SIMPLY THREAD ON TO THE CORNERS AND PUSH UP AS HIGH AS FABRIC ALLOWS

C.

- TAKE THE MEASUREMENTS OF 1 – 2 – 3 ON TABLE AND DRAW THE PIECES ON YOUR GRAPH PAPER — ALLOW SEAM ALLOWANCES ON EVERY EDGE. PIN, BASTE AND SEW TOGETHER — CUT AWAY EXCESS CLOTH IN THE CORNERS

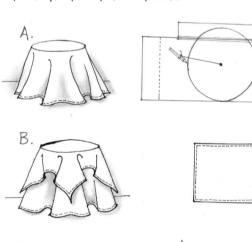

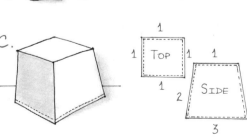

Screens

BE ADVENTUROUS –
EXPERIMENT A LITTLE!

LACE SCREEN – PERHAPS
MORE A ROOM DIVIDER

CURTAIN
RECIPES

Screen
Instructions

123

Instructions

A. STRIP THE SCREEN DOWN TO ITS WOODEN FRAME – STAPLE THE FABRIC TO THE FRAME PULLING IT AS TIGHT AS POSSIBLE

COVER THE STAPLES WITH YOUR RIBBON – USE A FABRIC GLUE

HAMMER IN YOUR ANTIQUE STUDS

B. SIMPLY TURN OVER THE TOP OF YOUR LACE PANEL – CUT A STRIP OF NEUTRAL COLOURED FABRIC AS A FACING – ABOUT 5CM (2") WIDE X WIDTH OF LACE – AND MAKE A POCKET FOR THE CURTAIN ROD. SLIP STITCH BOTH SIDES

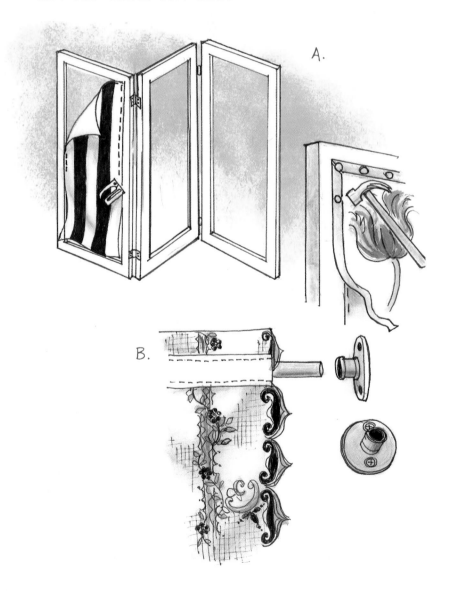

A.

B.

+ Templates

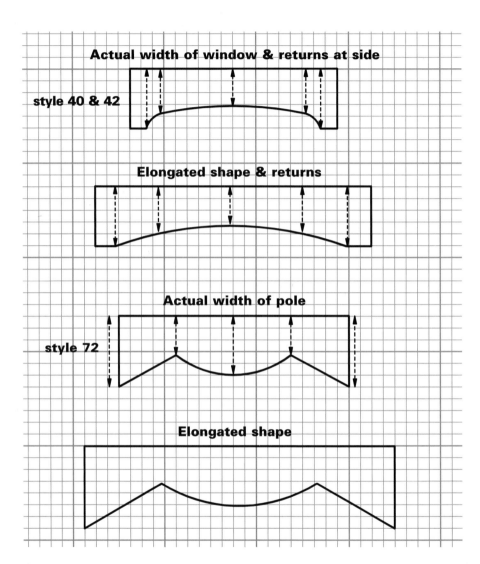

Actual width of window & returns at side

style 40 & 42

Elongated shape & returns

Actual width of pole

style 72

Elongated shape

REMEMBER AS THESE VALENCES ARE GATHERED YOU HAVE TO ELONGATE THE SHAPES TO ALLOW FOR THE FABRIC FULLNESS, SO YOU NEED TO CUT A SECOND TEMPLATE TO THE FINISHED SIZE OF THE VALANCE BEFORE GATHERING. THEN YOU NEED TO TAKE MEASUREMENTS AS INDICATED IN DIAGRAM 1 & TRANSFER TO DIAGRAM 2 IN ORDER TO GET THE SHAPE

LOOK FOR...

TEA TOWELS (LES TOURCHONS) APPEARED FIRST IN THE 13TH CENTURY — CRISP AND SIMPLE, OFF WHITE WITH RED INITIALS MODESTLY CROSS-STITCHED IN THE CORNER. IN THE 19TH CENTURY GIRLS WOULD EMBROIDER THEIR OWN INITIALS IN THE CORNER AND WHEN THEY WERE GETTING MARRIED THEY WOULD ADD THEIR FIANCES' INITIALS BESIDE THEIRS!

PROVENCIAL FABRICS (LES INDIENNES) ELECTRIC COLOURED PRINTS ORIGINALLY MADE IN INDIA, HAND BLOCKED AND COLOURED WITH VEGETABLE DYE. THEY BECAME VERY POPULAR IN THE 60S AND 70S COPIED BY SOULEIDO, WHO REVIVED THEM BUT NOW PERHAPS A LITTLE PASSÉ

LINENS (LE LINGE) WHITE OR OFF WHITE — BEAUTIFULLY EMBROIDERED AND EDGED WITH INTRICATE LACES. VERY COLLECTABLE — LOOK FOR TEA TOWELS, PILLOW CASES AND TABLE CLOTHS — ALL CAN BE ADAPTED INTO WINDOW COVERINGS PURE MAGIC

WHERE TO GO...

IF YOU LIVE IN FRANCE, AS I DO, YOU WILL FIND EVERY LITTLE VILLAGE HAS ITS OWN MARKET DAY. HERE ARE A FEW THAT I KNOW:

NICE — EVERY MONDAY BIG ANTIQUE MARKET — VERY GOOD

VALBONNE — 1ST SUNDAY IN EVERY MONTH — 3 VERY GOOD LINEN STALLS

ST TROPEZ — EVERY SATURDAY LARGE MARKET WORTH A VISIT

ANTIBES — SATURDAY MORNINGS

AIX-EN-PROVENCE — SATURDAYS ARE BEST — WORTH A VISIT

L'ISLE-SUR-SORGE — SUNDAYS — WONDERFUL TILES TOO

CANNES — 1ST SUNDAY OF EACH MONTH

PARIS — PUCES DE ST OUEN (PORTE DE CLIGNANCOURT) WONDERFUL FLEA MARKET SATURDAY, SUNDAY & MONDAY

UK SHOPS

LUNN ANTIQUES — KINGS ROAD, LONDON SW6

DIERDRE'S SHOP — TALBOT WALK — RIPLEY, SURREY

TOBIAS & THE ANGEL — WHITE HART LANE, LONDON, SW13

MARKETS

PORTOBELLO MARKET — PORTOBELLO ROAD, LONDON W11 — SATURDAYS BEST

KEMPTON RACE COURSE MARKET — SUNBURY, SURREY — 2ND & LAST TUESDAY EACH MONTH 01932 782 292

SANDOWN RACECOURSE MARKET — ESHER, SURREY — 0171 249 4050

THE 3 BELOW ARE SPONSORED BY THE DAILY MAIL. FOR DETAILS CALL 01636702 326

ARDINGLY — SUSSEX ● NEWARK — LINCOLNSHIRE ● MALVERN — WORCESTERSHIRE

Glossary
The Meaning Of Things

The Meaning Of Things

ARCHITRAVE MOULDING AROUND A DOOR OR WINDOW

BACKSTITCH A METHOD OF SEWING WITH OVERLAPPING STITCHES – SEE PAGE 11

BASTE A RUNNING STITCH – TACKING

BATTEN WOODEN SUPPORT FOR BLINDS

BLANKET STITCH A STITCH USED FOR EDGING

BRACKET WOODEN OR METAL SUPPORT FOR POLES OR BLINDS

BUCKRAM A COARSE FABRIC USED FOR STIFFENING THE TOPS OF CURTAINS OR BLINDS

CAFÉ CURTAIN CURTAIN USED FOR PRIVACY

CLEAT A HOOK TO TIE CORD ON TO – USED FOR BLINDS

DRAPES (US) CURTAINS (UK)

EYELET HOLE A METAL HOLE PUNCHED INTO FABRIC WITH AN EYELET MACHINE

FACING A STRIP OF FABRIC USED TO COVER RAW EDGES

FRENCH SEAM A DOUBLE SEAM WHICH ENCLOSES A RAW EDGE

GOBLET HEADING ALSO CALLED A TULIP HEADING – IS THE SAME AS A PINCH PLEAT BUT NOT PINCHED TOGETHER

HEADING TAPE TAPES WHICH CAN BE BOUGHT IN THE STORES USED TO GATHER THE TOP OF THE CURTAINS

HEM THE TURN UP AT THE BOTTOM OF A PAIR OF CURTAINS OR A BLIND

HERRINGBONE STITCH USED TO NEATEN THE EDGE OF FABRIC

ITALIAN STRINGING A METHOD OF PULLING BACK/AND UP A CURTAIN BY MEANS OF STRINGING IN A PARTICULAR WAY – SEE PAGE 35

LEADING EDGE THE CENTRE EDGES OF A PAIR OF CURTAINS

LINING A SECONDARY FABRIC USED TO BACK THE MAIN CURTAIN FABRIC

LOCK STITCH A STITCH USED TO JOIN THE LINING OR INTERLINING THE MAIN FABRIC

MITRE THE DIAGONAL JOIN OF 2 PIECES OF FABRIC FORMED AT A CORNER

PELMET A PIECE OF FABRIC WHICH IS ATTACHED TO A PELMET BOARD, LIKE A SKIRT

PENCIL PLEAT IS A NEAT PENCIL – LIKE PLEAT AT THE TOP OF CURTAINS

POCKET HEADING (UK) ROD POCKET (USA)

POLE A WOODEN OR METAL ROD FROM WHICH A CURTAIN HANGS

PORTIÉRE ROD A SPECIALLY MADE THIN POLE WHICH SWINGS THROUGH 180 DEGREES.

RAW EDGE THE ROUGH CUT EDGE OF FABRICS

RECESS WHERE BLINDS OR CURTAINS ARE FIXED IN THE ALCOVE OF A WINDOW

ROMAN BLIND A FABRIC BLIND WHICH IS OPERATED BY A SERIES OF STRINGS AT THE BACK AND ALLOWS BLIND TO FOLD NEATLY OVER A WINDOW

SELVEDGE A NARROW STRIP ON THE EDGE OF FABRICS TO PREVENT FRAYING

SHEERS (VOILES OR NETS UK) A FINE TRANSLUCENT FABRIC

SLIP STITCH USED TO STITCH THE FOLDING EDGE OF A FABRIC TO ANOTHER

STACK BACK A PLACE WHERE CURTAINS CAN REST WITHOUT BLOCKING THE LIGHT I.E. EITHER SIDE OF THE WINDOW

TAB A NARROW WIDTH OF FABRIC WHICH WHEN TURNED OVER DOUBLED FORMS A LOOP

TEMPLATE A PATTERN CUT FROM PAPER OR CARD WHICH IS USED TO MARK A SPECIFIC OUTLINE ON A PIECE OF FABRIC

TRIMMING PASSEMENTERIE – SEE PAGE 20

VALANCE A GATHERED PIECE OF FABRIC WHICH IS ATTACHED GENERALLY TO A PELMET BOARD

VOILE (UK) SHEERS (USA) – TRANSLUCENT FABRIC

Sources
UK Suppliers

FABRICS – TELEPHONE FOR
NEAREST STOCKIST

ANNA FRENCH
020 7351 1126

ANDREW MARTIN
020 7225 5100

BRIAN YATES
020 7352 0123

CATH KIDSTON
020 7221 4248

CHASE ERWIN
020 7352 7271

COLEFAX & FOWLER
020 7244 7427

CONRAN
020 7589 7401

DESIGNERS' GUILD
020 7351 5775

IAN MANKIN
020 77220997

IKEA
020 8208 5600

JANE CHURCHILL
020 7730 9847

JOHN LEWIS
020 7629 7711

KA (*BRANCHES WORLD WIDE)
020 7584 7952

LAURA ASHLEY
0870 562 2116

MALABAR
020 7501 4200

OSBORNE & LITTLE
020 7352 1456

PONGEES
020 7739 9130

ROBERT ALLEN
01494 474741

TURNELL & GIGON
020 8971 1711 (SCHUMACHER)

ZIMMER & RHODE
020 7351 7115

Z BUTT (DENIM & CALICO)
020 7247 7776

TRIMMINGS

BRITISH TRIMMINGS
0161 480 6122

JOHN LEWIS
020 7629 7711

JANE CHURCHILL
020 7361 0666

WENDY CUSHING
020 7351 5796

WEMYSS (HOULES)
020 7225 3305

V V ROULEAUX
020 7730 3125

POLES & TRACKING

BRADLEYS
01449 722 724

COPE & TIMMINS
0845 458 8860

JOHN LEWIS (RETAIL)
020 7828 1000

McCULLOCH + WALLIS (RETAIL)
020 7629 0311

McKINNEY
020 7627 5077

PRICES & CO
01273 421 999

USA Suppliers

FABRICS — THESE ARE TRADE OUTLETS BUT YOU CAN CALL FOR YOUR NEAREST STOCKIST

Anna French
617 574 9030

Cath Kidston
212 751 3333

Colefax & Fowler
212 753 4488

Designers Guild
212 751 3333

Jane Churchill
212 753 4488

Osborne & Little
212 751 3333

Robert Allen
1 800 333 3777

Schumacher
212 415 3900

Waverley
1 800 423 5881

Zimmer and Rohde
212 627 8880

SPECIALIST STORES
ABC carpet and home
212 473 3000

Beckstenstein's fabrics & interiors, 4 West 20th St. New York

Calico corners
610 444 9700

Gracious Homes
212 231 7800

Home Depot Expo
770 433 8211

Jo-Ann
330 463 6790

TRIMMINGS
Samuel & sons — (trade)
212 704 8000

Conso Products
(trade inexpensive)
864. 427 9004

Houles
212 935 3900

Jane Churchill
212 753 4488

Robert Allen
1 800 333 3777

HABADASHERY STORES
Beckenstein's Fabrics & interiors
4 West 20th Street, New York

Gracious Homes
212 231 7800

HARDWARE
ABC carpet & home
212 473 3000

Calico corners
610 444 9700

Gracious home
212 231 7800

Home depot Expo
770 433 8211

Jo-Ann
330 463 6790

Robert Allen
1 800 333 3777